AT THE
MOVIES

AT THE
MOVIES

BEHIND THE BIG SCREEN

THE HISTORY, SCANDALS, DIRECTORS, STUDIOS AND STARS

DON SHIACH

southwater

This edition is published by Southwater

Southwater is an imprint of Anness Publishing Ltd
Hermes House, 88–89 Blackfriars Road, London SE1 8HA
tel. 020 7401 2077; fax 020 7633 9499
www.southwaterbooks.com; info@anness.com

© Anness Publishing Ltd 2005

UK agent: The Manning Partnership Ltd
6 The Old Dairy, Melcombe Road, Bath BA2 3LR
tel. 01225 478444; fax 01225 478440; sales@manning-partnership.co.uk

UK distributor: Grantham Book Services Ltd
Isaac Newton Way, Alma Park Industrial Estate, Grantham, Lincs NG31 9SD
tel. 01476 541080; fax 01476 541061; orders@gbs.tbs-ltd.co.uk

North American agent/distributor: National Book Network
4501 Forbes Boulevard, Suite 200, Lanham, MD 20706
tel. 301 459 3366; fax 301 429 5746; www.nbnbooks.com

Australian agent/distributor: Pan Macmillan Australia
Level 18, St Martins Tower, 31 Market St, Sydney, NSW 2000
tel. 1300 135 113; fax 1300 135 103; customer.service@macmillan.com.au

New Zealand agent/distributor: David Bateman Ltd
30 Tarndale Grove, Off Bush Road, Albany, Auckland
tel. (09) 415 7664; fax (09) 415 8892

A CIP catalogue record for this book is available from the British Library.

Publisher: Joanna Lorenz
Editorial Director: Judith Simons
Project Editor: Felicity Forster
Designer: Peter Bailey–Proof Books
Cover designer: Chloë Steers
Prepress: Paul Beadle
Production Controller: Claire Rae

Previously published as part of a larger volume, *The Movies*

1 3 5 7 9 10 8 6 4 2

CONTENTS

CONTENTS

FOREWORD

It is difficult to believe that back in the 1950s, when the movie business was hit hard by the advent of television and other competing mass entertainments, the death of the movies – or, at least, of the habit of going to the movies – was confidently forecast by many an expert. Fifty years ago, very few would have predicted, as we entered the new millennium, that cinema would be very much alive and well and a multi-billion-dollar enterprise across the globe. Certainly, the film business has changed enormously in the last few decades, as most people now see their movies in their own homes via satellite and cable television, videos and DVDs rather than in a cinema. But somehow the magic of movie-going lives on. Blockbuster movies can make enormous profits for their producers not only from box-office receipts around the world, but also from sales and rentals of videos and DVDs and the revenue from showings on television. New cinema technology

ABOVE *Gainsborough melodramas such as* The Wicked Lady *were the cinematic equivalent of bodice-rippers in books, but they made stars of British actors such as James Mason and Margaret Lockwood.*

will further transform the way we have movies delivered to us. For example, the days of celluloid distribution are surely numbered: soon movies on first release will be "pumped into" thousands of cinemas by cable distribution. All in all, the rumour circulating back in the 1950s about the death of the cinema proved to be much exaggerated.

It seems, too, that each new generation falls in love with the products of old Hollywood, the British film industry at its peak, as well as the great works of European cinema, revelling in Astaire–Rogers musicals such as *Top Hat* and *Carefree*, the great MGM musicals, suffering with Margaret Lockwood and James Mason in those laughable Gainsborough melodramas such as *The Wicked Lady* and *Jassy*, laughing with Buster Keaton or Cary Grant in Hollywood comedies such as *The Navigator* and *Bringing Up Baby*, solving murder mysteries with *The*

Thin Man and partners, weeping at *Casablanca* or empathizing with Jean Gabin or Marcello Mastroianni in great European classics such *La Grande Illusion* or *8½*. Old movies will never die; they will eternally resurface on television until the last moments of human history.

Hollywood in its heyday, with its excesses and absurdities, its real achievements and its crass failures of taste and artistic judgement, has gone forever. But the movie business regularly regenerates itself, discovering new and unexpected forms. The Hollywood studio system has long since disappeared, but new stars (not only star actors but star directors, producers and screenwriters) are constantly being created by a business that devours and spits out talents, or even non-talents, who prove their worth by making a buck for the owners. New niche markets for different types of movies are always being identified and catered for: the teen movie, the over-40s movie, the gross-out comedy, the adult cartoon movie, the special effects extravaganza and many more. Movies are very big business, and enormous riches await those, like

ABOVE *Fan magazines were eagerly read and stars such as the young Joan Bennett were promoted on their covers as iconic beauties.*

ABOVE Bringing Up Baby *was one of the most successful of the type of madcap, irrational comedies that came to be known as "screwball".*

ABOVE *The movie villain of all movie villains, Darth Vader, in the Star Wars movies. George Lucas, the guiding creative hand behind the series, became a major Hollywood player because of the success of the first movie in 1977.*

ABOVE *8½ (1963) was Fellini's reflections on his own career as a director after having made eight and a half movies. For Fellini fans this is a key film of the Italian master.*

Steven Spielberg, George Lucas or James Cameron, who tap into the public consciousness. Movies are spectacle, they are dreams, they are a view of reality and unreality, a world

ABOVE *For many people, it is movies such as* Casablanca, *a prime example of a "bad good movie", that define the magic and enduring appeal of the cinema.*

of fantasy, an escape, a Utopia. They inhabit a separate universe of their own. Cinema, for better or worse, was the dominant art form of the 20th century and may well be the same in the 21st century as well. Even the fiercest detractors of this mass entertainment would have to admit that movies touch the lives of more

people on this planet than books, music or theatre do. There is no escaping them.

This book attempts to encapsulate something of the appeal of the movies. By its very nature, it has had to be a selective process; after all, no two movie fans would agree on a list of favourite stars, most important directors or best movies. Hollywood and its products figure most prominently because the history of movies is largely the history of the American film industry, although that is not to deny the importance of other major film-producing nations. Indeed, more certainly does not always mean better, as is all too obvious from some of the lamentable excesses of the Hollywood machine. The American film industry now dominates the world film market to an extent that the old Hollywood moguls such as Louis B. Mayer and Jack Warner only dreamt about. This is not altogether a healthy aspect of contemporary cinema. The French defend their native film industry from the swamping effects of American movies. I wish other countries such as Britain would follow suit.

If you are reading this, you are almost certainly a movie fan – maybe even a movie buff. You belong to a universal club with millions of members across the globe, all in love with a technological medium that has harnessed the stuff of which dreams are made. Whenever people get together and spend time reminiscing, at some stage the topic of favourite movies will come up. Many of our most common cultural references are related to movies. The USA even elected a former minor movie star as one of its presidents. Hollywood, indeed, has a lot to answer for, as well as plenty to be proud of. So, as Dorothy Parker once put it:

OH, COME MY LOVE AND
JOIN WITH ME,
THE OLDEST INFANT INDUSTRY.
COME SEEK THE BOURNE
OF PALM AND PEARL,
THE LOVELY LAND OF
BOY-MEETS-GIRL.

COME GRACE THIS
LOTUS-LADEN SHORE,
THE ISLE OF
DO-WHAT'S-DONE BEFORE.
COME CURB THE NEW AND
WATCH THE OLD WIN,
BUT WHERE THE STREETS ARE
PAVED WITH GOLDWYN.

7

THE HISTORY OF THE MOVIES

THE MOVIE industry entered the new
millennium in fairly robust health
despite many gloomy forecasts that the
movie-going experience was on its last legs.
Most of us nowadays do indeed see most movies
through television, videos and DVDs, but
the tradition of "going to the pictures" has not
disappeared entirely. The cinema started out
as a shared experience and let us hope that it
continues to be one. In this section we trace the
development of the movie-going experience.

LEFT *The famous chariot race from the 1959 version of Ben-Hur.*
Charlton Heston beat Stephen Boyd in a race that was fixed.

INTRODUCTION

The film industry has existed for well over a hundred years now and, of course, has been transformed in ways that could not possibly have been foreseen from the perspective of the early days of the 1890s. The history of the cinema reflects the changing economic, industrial/post-industrial and sociological structures of a whole century. The entertainment business, of which the movies are such an important part, has grown to staggering proportions such that it plays a central role in the business life of many nations. If we all ceased going to the movies or stopped watching them on television, video or DVD, then the economy of the world would be in serious trouble.

What is essential to remember about the film industry is that it is an industry and movies are the result of a technological and industrial process that no other art form requires. Indeed, it is the fact that films are produced through this technological process that allows cultural snobs to look down on movies as cultural artefacts. Cinema has always had to contend with this kind of disparagement from people who prefer theatre or literature, and the fact that movies need really big bucks from investors before they can be made also allows movie-haters to sneer. How can anything worthwhile emerge from an industry where the dread hand of commerce controls the process, they ask? Well, somehow or other, good movies do get made, as well as lots of commercial dross.

From the early days of cinema, serious followers of this new technological art had to plough a largely lonely furrow in their admiration for the movies. Even as the movies enter the second century of their existence, there are still many people who will willingly sit through all kinds of second-rate nonsense in the theatre and think they are watching something worthwhile because it is, after all, the theatre, while dismissing the movies as mindless entertainment. But these are the dwindling minority. Movies have had to fight long and hard to be taken as seriously as books, theatre, art objects and music but, for the most part, that battle has been won. The once-derided pastime for the moronic masses has achieved much in its domination of the arts. How, then, did the cinema reach this pre-eminent position in the cultural life of millions of people around the world?

THE HUMBLE BEGINNINGS

The international film market we know today grew from the kinetoscope: a simple machine comprising a cabinet and a length of film on a spool. The customers inserted a coin, the light shone and the film was projected on to the back of the cabinet. From our 21st century perspective, it doesn't seem much of a show, but it must have seemed like magic then.

Movies have always been perceived as an American product but, in fact, European inventors played crucial roles in the development of the cinematic apparatus: for example, William Friese-Green in England, Georges Demeny in France, and Ottomar Anschutz and Max Skladanowsky in Germany. In the 1890s the pioneers were French: the Lumière brothers, Gaumont and Pathé.

ABOVE *An advert for the Lumière brothers' shows in Paris. To a turn of the century audience, these Lumière extravaganzas had more than a touch of magic about them, an expectation the brothers skilfully exploited.*

However, it was in America that the public showing of early movies rapidly grew. Kinetoscope parlours were opened in 1894 in the principal cities of America. Perhaps it is not absolutely accurate to say that cinema began with the kinetoscope, because the essence of the cinematic experience is its communal nature (while retaining privacy for the individuals sitting in the darkness of the cinema as they see their dreams appear before them). Thus, the cinema was really born with the invention of a projector that could throw a series of moving images on to a screen. The Latham brothers and W.K.L. Dickson invented the Panoptikon projector, which took movies out of the kinetoscope

cabinet, and in September 1895 in Paris the Lumière brothers showed a paying audience films that they themselves had produced in their Lyons factory.

In the USA, musical theatres began to present movies as part of their variety bills. Film companies were formed – the Biograph and Vitagraph companies, for example. In 1902 the first motion picture theatre, the Electric, was opened in Los Angeles. Early cinemas were called "nickelodeons" because you paid a nickel (five cents) to see the show. By 1907 there were approximately 3000 such nickelodeons across America. The cinema was on its way to becoming

ABOVE *A contemporary artist's impression of a kinetoscope parlour in America. Note the respectable ambience and the genteel decor that seek to reinforce the notion that such establishments are quite "proper" for ladies and gentlemen.*

big business and despite dips in public favour, for example during the Depression of the 1930s and advent of the television age in the 1950s, it would never be anything other than a major industry thereafter.

THE NARRATIVE FILM

New York was at this time the centre of American film-making; Hollywood was still a suburb of Los Angeles that was kind to oranges. However, in 1903 the Edison factory produced a landmark in cinematic history – the first true narrative film, *The Great Train Robbery*. At the Biograph Studios in New York a few years later a young actor, Lawrence Griffith, replaced a sick director on a one-reeler, *The Adventures of Dollie*, and

launched the career of D.W. Griffith, film director. If the young Griffith had had any pretensions at this stage of his career to being a "serious artist", then he must have had to lay them aside, because between 1908 and 1913 he directed 450 motion pictures. The vast majority of these movies have not survived because they were disposable merchandise, produced to seduce the punters into the movie houses and then disposed of. The nickelodeons

RIGHT AND BELOW *The emblems of the Vitagraph and Essanay Studios.*

at this time were very hungry monsters with a bottomless appetite for 15- or 30-minute features to set before an eager mass audience. Films were cranked off the assembly line one after the other. Several movies would be shot cheek-by-jowl on crowded stages in the early studios. After all, there was no dialogue to speak, no sound effects to be recorded. These were the silents.

LEFT *It's a long, long way to* Dances with Wolves, *but* The Great Train Robbery *(1903) was not only the first full-length narrative film but also the first western to have them queueing round the block.*

THE PATH TO *THE BIRTH OF A NATION*

By 1912 "proper" cinemas, as opposed to nickelodeons or halls, were fairly common and admission prices had doubled. Commensurate with this increase in admission prices was the increased length of the movies shown: one- and two-reelers of 15 or 30 minutes had given way to four- and five-reelers. Motion pictures were moving up in the world. One of the first entrepreneurs to realize this was Adolph Zukor, who founded the Famous Players Film Company.

Gradually, he and other entrepreneurs seduced famous stage actors away from the stage and on to the screen.

However, American films had hot competition from abroad. For example, the Italian-made *Quo Vadis?*, an eight-reel epic, ran for 22 weeks in New York.

Hollywood began to replace New York as the centre of film-making. The reasons were several: independent producers went west to escape the clutches of the Motion Picture Patents Company, a trust (including the Vitagraph and Biograph companies) formed to enforce a monopoly on film-making patents; the suburbs around Los Angeles were relatively undeveloped and furnished excellent natural resources for film-making on the cheap (sun, desert, mountains, nearby urban locations); and, crucially, the area was also a source of far cheaper labour than could be found in New York.

In 1914 the Jesse Lasky Feature Play Company was formed. Lasky's brother-in-law, Samuel Goldfish, later Goldwyn, joined the company, as did another famous Hollywood name, Cecil B. De Mille, who directed their first feature *The Squaw Man* in a barn. In the same year Paramount Pictures was formed to release the pictures of

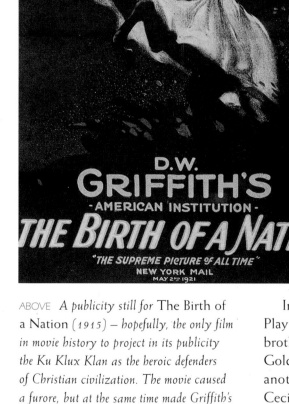

ABOVE *A publicity still for* The Birth of a Nation *(1915) – hopefully, the only film in movie history to project in its publicity the Ku Klux Klan as the heroic defenders of Christian civilization. The movie caused a furore, but at the same time made Griffith's reputation as a major innovator in terms of film technique. And, yes, it made megabucks at the box office too.*

ABOVE *Yes, this was the humble beginning of the major studio, Warner Brothers. Even today, Hollywood and Los Angeles have a certain air of impermanence about them, but these premises look like they would not have survived a strong wind, let alone the mildest of Californian earth tremors.*

the Famous Players Company. Production, distribution and exhibition were the three battlegrounds for the early companies.

In 1915 arguably the most famous silent movie of all, *The Birth of a Nation*, was released. A 12-reel epic about the civil war and its aftermath, the movie, directed by D.W. Griffith, was the first film to be granted "road show" status. It was a huge box-office hit all over the world and won critical praise from sources which had hitherto scorned the movies as "dreams for the masses".

The Birth of a Nation also aroused great controversy and opposition, particularly from black people. From our historical perspective, we can see just how horrendously racist it was in its ideology. The Ku Klux Klan were represented heroically as the defenders of civilized values, and carpetbaggers and rapacious "negroes" as the villains of the piece. However, Griffith's advanced film techniques – close-ups, crosscutting, the staging of elaborate crowd and battle scenes – indicated that the cinema had made a huge technical advance.

12

AMERICAN DOMINATION OF THE WORLD MARKET

By the end of World War I the American film industry had effectively established itself as the dominant cinema, although the film industries of the Soviet Union, Germany, France and Scandinavia would challenge Hollywood in the 1920s in terms of the artistic use of the medium. Directors such as Fritz Lang, Sergei Eisenstein, Friedrich Murnau, Abel Gance, Jean Renoir,

after film in the sure knowledge that American box-office revenues alone would produce substantial profits. Foreign revenues were the icing on the cake. Exhibitors all around the world were clamouring for products to show, and the USA produced far more films than anywhere else.

The businessmen who owned the studios realized that there were three crucial areas of the film business they

showing their own products and all revenues came back to the parent company. Most of the early movie moguls came into film production via other business activities as diverse as theatre ownership and scrap-dealing, and they brought a hard-nosed, ruthless, market-orientated approach to the enterprise of making movies for a mass audience.

The American film industry was also very efficient at publicizing its wares. The studios were adept at creating an aura of glamour and excitement around movies, and stars were the main carriers of this aura. The production of glamour was aided and abetted by newspapers and magazines in all the developed countries of the world. Thus, when Douglas Fairbanks and Mary Pickford came to Europe after the end of the World War I, they were greeted by enormous numbers of people wherever they went. Movie stars were the new royalty, and a huge publicity machine, partly wielded by the

ABOVE *D.W. Griffith directed* Hearts of the World *at the request of the British government who wanted a propaganda film to boost morale. Griffith duly obliged.*

Mauritz Stiller and Carl Dreyer made films that very few American film-makers could match. However, to ruthless movie executives films are pure business. Studios had the power to impose their products wherever films were shown commercially.

Their own huge domestic market gave American film-makers an enormous advantage over other countries. Studios could make film

had to control if they were to establish a virtual monopoly in the marketplace: production, distribution and exhibition. Of these, the real money was to be made in distribution and exhibition, so all the major Hollywood studios were intent on setting up their distribution arms and buying as many cinemas in prime locations as they could. As the distributors of their own films, they could charge a substantial rental (usually between 30 and 40 per cent of box-office receipts) to cinemas not owned by themselves. As the owners of their own cinemas, they were

ABOVE *Mary Pickford was more than just a pretty face. When her film career waned, she proved her worth as a movie mogul.*

ABOVE *Douglas Fairbanks was a major swashbuckling star of the silent era.*

Hollywood studios and partly by other media with vested interests in aiding this publicity, made sure they would retain that aura for years to come.

It was not only stars that projected this aura. Important movie-makers such as Griffith and De Mille were quickly recognized by the producers as "brand names" to sell their product. However, it was stars such as Fairbanks, Valentino, Garbo, Ronald Colman, Vilma Banky, Theda Bara and many others that the producers ultimately banked on to bring the customers in – the

stars, and the easily recognizable type of product movie-goers were drawn to see again and again: westerns, exotic romantic dramas, swashbucklers, slapstick comedies, thrillers, cops-and-robber thrillers and musicals.

By the early 1920s, the American film industry had settled on the formula that would stand it in good stead (with troughs along the way) over the next decades: provide a steady diet of mainly undemanding, populist entertainments manufactured by assembly-line production methods with the stars that people loved and the content that customers would identify as the type of picture they preferred to see. Art was not part of the equation; if art happened by accident in the process of making a motion picture, that was beneficial to the prestige of the industry as long as it didn't put off the paying customers.

ABOVE *Two of the silent screen's biggest stars, Ronald Colman and Vilma Banky in a typical romantic melodrama of the 1920s. The vast commercial success of the movies led to an explosion in the number of related publications that exploited this mass interest in the new art. This souvenir supplement issued by* Picture Show *magazine illustrates this.*

LEFT *Her acting abilities may be in dispute, but for her many fans, Greta Garbo remains the eternal goddess of the silver screen. Publicists worked very hard to create this illusion.*

THE MAGIC OF THE MOVIES

By the 1920s movies were very big business indeed. The average movie product was unsophisticated and direct in its appeal, whether it was a Chaplin or Mack Sennett comedy or a melodramatic tearjerker starring Gloria Swanson or Norma Talmadge. Film-makers went after family audiences because that was where the money was, so escapism was the order of the day. The showmen's belief was that the movies should offer harmless entertainment and not bother with "messages". Movies offered an escape from everyday problems: they transported you to exotic locations and embroiled you in romantic and dangerous exploits. Up there on the screen, you could watch the parting of the Red Sea (courtesy of Cecil B. De Mille), see Ramon Novarro win a chariot race in Ancient Rome, or witness the crucifixion of Christ in *The King of Kings*. Spectacle, mayhem and melodrama are the stuff of which dreams are made, and the movies sold dreams.

The Hollywood studios were the Dream Factories, manufacturing fantasy for the millions. Dream Factories required Dream Palaces in which these manufactured dreams could be experienced, and so exotic cinemas such as Grauman's Chinese Theater in Los Angeles, the Granada in humble Tooting in South London, or Radio City Music Hall in New York were built in the years to come to add an extra enticement to cinema-goers. Movies transported you to a different world, so it was appropriate that cinemas should have this other-worldly ambience, as well.

ABOVE *Charlie Chaplin's popularity continued well after he had ceased producing the comedies that made him famous. This is a Belgian poster for a "portamanteau" 1950s movie of some of the best Chaplin comedy routines. All over the world, Chaplin was probably the most instantly recognized movie icon.*

LEFT *Buster Keaton is many people's favourite silent-era comedian. His career virtually vanished with the coming of sound. Lovers of silent movie comedies are usually as diehard as traditional jazz fans – and just as purist.*

THE COMING OF SOUND AND THE DEPRESSION

Although movies had become established as a major entertainment form worldwide, by the mid-1920s audiences were beginning to decrease. Films such as *Ben-Hur* and *The Ten Commandments* still made a fortune for their makers, but for the run-of-the-mill product, audiences were becoming harder to find. Just as it looked as though cinema's advance might be checked, the cavalry, in the shape of Warner Brothers and Vitaphone, came riding over the horizon, bugles blowing, to the rescue. Movies with sound had already been tried in a series of Vitaphone shorts and a musical accompaniment and sound effects in the John Barrymore version of *Don Juan*, but the major studios had turned their backs on this technological innovation because of the cost of installing equipment. But the Warner brothers – Harry, Jack, Sam and Albert – took a chance on Vitaphone because they needed a new impetus if they were going to be able to force their way into theatre ownership, which was so crucial if you wanted to become a major player on the Hollywood stage. The brothers backed *The Jazz Singer* with Al Jolson blacking up, and it made millions. The end was nigh for silent movies and every studio in Hollywood clambered on the bandwagon that Warners had set in motion. The headstart they had in producing "talkies" catapulted Warner Brothers to major studio status and forced their rivals to catch up.

They talk! They sing! They have sound effects! Movie-makers turned to musicals to make the most of this new technological development. During

ABOVE *Ronald Colman was one silent screen star whose career survived into the sound era, but his co-star here, Lili Damita, was not so lucky when the "talkies" took over.*

the first couple of years of the talkies, the market was saturated with all-singing, all-talking, all-dancing musical extravaganzas like *The Hollywood Revue of 1929*, *Broadway Melody*, *The Desert Song*, *Show of Shows* and *Gold Diggers of Broadway*. Producers also turned to filming Broadway stage shows, which was easy and relatively cheap. However, the essence of movies is that they move, and so audiences soon tired of these stage-bound exercises. A surfeit of musicals also led to audience indifference. And the Wall Street Crash had heralded the start of the Depression – millions of people around the world were struggling to survive and had no extra money to indulge in the purchase of movie tickets. The movie industry faced an extremely hard task in enticing Depression audiences into the emptying cinemas.

ABOVE The Hollywood Revue of 1929 *was a precursor of MGM's great musicals. Its static production numbers and corny routines paved the way for more sophisticated fare less than a decade later.*

GANGSTERS, MOLLS AND CENSORSHIP

In the early part of the 1930s, Hollywood turned to sensationalist drama to attract customers back into the cinemas. Three gangster films made in 1931–32, *Little Caesar*, *The Public Enemy* and *Scarface*, were successes both commercially and artistically, but aroused opposition from pressure groups such as the American Legion and Daughters of the American Revolution. These films portrayed the underbelly of the American Dream, a distorted Horatio Alger morality tale of success. The methods used by Edward G. Robinson, James Cagney and Paul Muni in these movies to achieve power in their gangland underworld had more than a passing resemblance to the ruthless machinations of American big business, and this did not endear them to the establishment. Law enforcers were portrayed as at best incompetent and at worst corrupt and this, too, irritated those who cherished the idea of the

ABOVE *Edward G. Robinson found instant screen immortality when he played an Al Capone-type gangster in* Little Caesar. *He impersonated criminals convincingly and won himself a huge fan following.*

Republic as the land of opportunity for decent American citizens who played it by the rules.

The other ingredient used by producers to tempt customers back into the cinemas was sex. Although extremely mild by present-day standards, movies such as *Dishonored* and *Morocco* with Marlene Dietrich and *The Story of Temple Drake* with Florence Eldridge had puritans all over the country reaching for their writing pads to dash off a letter to their Congressman. Mae West's films, such as *Night After Night* and *She Done Him Wrong*, also produced strong reactions. Jean Harlow was another new star who courted, and gained, disapproval.

ABOVE *Jean Harlow became the "bad girl" of 1930s movies, symbolizing a type of brassy and unsubtle glamour.*

Hollywood studios sniffed the wind and recognized that, if they did not do something themselves, they might be faced with external censorship. In 1927 the Motion Pictures Producers and Distributors of America (MPPDA) had established a code to govern the making of motion pictures, but now this code was updated and an

ABOVE *James Cagney was another major star who impersonated gangsters on screen and won a huge fan following for doing so.*

office known as the Production Code Administration (PCA, but commonly called the Hays Office after MPPDA chief William Hays, then later the Breen Office) was given the responsibility for making sure that the studios obeyed it. All scripts had to be approved by the PCA before shooting started, and when the film was completed the PCA could insist on cuts by threatening to refuse its Seal of Approval. A film without the PCA Seal of Approval could not be shown in any cinema that came under the jurisdiction of the MPPDA. In fact, the major studios, which controlled the MPPDA, turned this situation to their own advantage, and used the Seal of Approval system to ward off competitors and independent producers. They not only controlled which films could be shown on the major circuits, but also had a stranglehold through the PCA on the content of American movies. The extreme puritanism of the PCA conveniently suited the studios' commercial needs. They were after an undemanding family audience, and used the code as their excuse to produce "harmless" and largely mindless movies that promoted "the American Way of Life".

Other genres that did well at the box office in the 1930s were horror films and musicals once again. A cycle of cheaply made flicks dealing with

the Dracula and Frankenstein myths made stars of Bela Lugosi, Boris Karloff and Lon Chaney Jnr. After its brief demise, the musical underwent a rebirth with a series of Warners "Depression" musicals directed by Busby Berkeley, the recipe for which was regimented battalions of sturdy chorus girls, Nuremberg Rally-type production numbers and opulent costumes and settings. More sophisticated were the series of Astaire–Rogers musicals with Art Deco settings and the effortless grace of the two stars. These musicals could safely be described as "harmless entertainment", an antidote to the grimness of the decade. It was also the decade of screwball and sophisticated comedies such as *His Girl Friday* and *The Philadelphia Story*. The Marx Brothers were at their peak and the Disney studios were hugely successful with colourful animated features such as *Snow White and the Seven Dwarfs*. In the midst of all this escapism, some films with a populist tone emerged to confront the social problems of the time: Frank Capra's *Mr Deeds Comes to Town* and *Mr Smith Goes to Washington*, Fritz Lang's *Fury*

ABOVE *More sophisticated comedy fare was served up by Cary Grant, Katharine Hepburn and James Stewart in* The Philadelphia Story.

and John Ford's *The Grapes of Wrath*. However, audiences continued to decline, despite the studios offering double bills to their customers and cinema-owners even offering free china and other give-aways to entice movie-goers.

In Britain, the Korda brothers were establishing a production company that would rival Hollywood studios with films such as *The Private Life of Henry the Eighth* and *The Four Feathers*. Britain was often in the vanguard of technical advance, such as the introduction of colour, and Michael Powell's movie, *The Thief of Bagdad* (1940) showed what British technicians could achieve under imaginative direction. However, as usual, most British cinema seemed to be stuck in the past. By contrast, French cinema, with talents such as Marcel Pagnol, Jean Renoir and Marcel Carné, produced memorable films such as *Marius, La Règle du Jeu, La Grande Illusion* and *Le Quai des Brumes*. Stalinist dictatorship had locked Soviet directors such as Eisenstein into serving the interests of the totalitarian state after the major achievement of *Battleship Potemkin*.

ABOVE *The Disney studio were pushing back the frontiers of animated film in full-length cartoons such as* Snow White and the Seven Dwarfs *(1937).*

WARTIME BOOM

Colour quickly caught on in the late 1930s, and on December 31, 1939, in Atlanta, Georgia, the première was held of the technicolor epic, *Gone with the Wind*, which would go on to be one of the box-office winners of all time. Once America had entered World War II, an economic boom followed. People had money to spend and audiences craved Hollywood's brand of escapism to help keep grim reality at bay. Musicals flourished once more, with stars such as Betty Grable, Judy Garland and Gene Kelly. The so-called "women's picture" took off, aimed at a predominantly female audience separated from lovers and husbands: *The Great Lie, Now Voyager* and *Mildred Pierce* were three of the more memorable of these melodramas. Orson Welles had

managed to make *Citizen Kane* and *The Magnificent Ambersons* before RKO and Hollywood realized they had a talented rebel on their hands. Humphrey Bogart became a megastar with *The Maltese Falcon* and *Casablanca*, which did Ingrid Bergman's career no

ABOVE *Bette Davis and Mary Astor co-starred in* The Great Lie, *one of the many "women's pictures" that Davis and others starred in during this period.*

ABOVE Gone with the Wind *premièred in Atlanta on December 31, 1939, and at the time it seemed the last word in spectacular screen action.*

harm either. The dark days of the war also saw the emergence of a group of films that critics later dubbed *"film noir"*. The wartime shortages of materials to build sets and the restriction on the use of lighting may have forced film-makers to employ shadowy lighting techniques and expressionist designs, but there was also something doom-laden in the air that lasted into peacetime and permeated classic *film noir* movies such as *The Dark Mirror, Crossfire, Double Indemnity* and *Out of the Past*. Britain, meanwhile, predictably produced morale-raising movies such

distribution arms. Now that incentive was being taken away from them by a government that had begun to move in this direction before the war had intervened.

The Anti-Trust Law, or the Paramount decree, in essence broke the studios' monopoly hold on all aspects of the film business. This, in tandem with a 50 per cent drop in audiences suffered by the industry in the 10 years after the peak of 1946, forced the break-up of the old studio system. "Old Hollywood" would, over the next 20 to 30 years, change into "new Hollywood", in which the names of Louis B. Mayer, Harry Cohn and other moguls became a distant reminder of the great old days.

as *San Demetrio-London*, *In Which We Serve* and *The Way to the Stars*; for the home front, the industry produced morale-boosters such as *Two Thousand Women*. At times, it seemed that only John Mills and David Niven stood between the country and defeat. France under German occupation still managed to produce the odd masterpiece, especially *Les Enfants du Paradis*.

The absolute peak year for audience attendance in America was 1946: there were 90 million admissions per week across the nation, a figure that the present-day industry cannot even remotely approach. Business would never be the same again, however, and from then on the film industry contracted.

There were two main causes of the decline in movie attendances. Firstly, in 1948 there was a great increase in the number of television sets sold in the USA; the relatively new phenomenon of television was now the cinema's greatest competitor. Television provided free entertainment in people's own homes – why bother to go out and pay good money to see a movie? World War II had interrupted the development of television as a mass medium, but now

in the immediate post-war years we were entering the television age.

A second most important factor in the decline of the American film industry was legislation passed by the US government to break up the virtual monopoly that the "Big Five" studios enjoyed within the industry. The 1948 Paramount Decree forced the studios to sell off their cinemas in the prime sites of the largest American cities. This was a body blow to the studios because, contrary to popular belief, it was in the spheres of exhibition and distribution that they made their real profits. Production was the third arm of the monopoly structure exercised by the studios, but the major studios made as many movies as they did primarily in order to service their own exhibition and

ABOVE *World War II continued to fascinate British film-makers.* San Demetrio-London *was an Ealing Studios production. These movies were propagandist in their tone and appeal.*

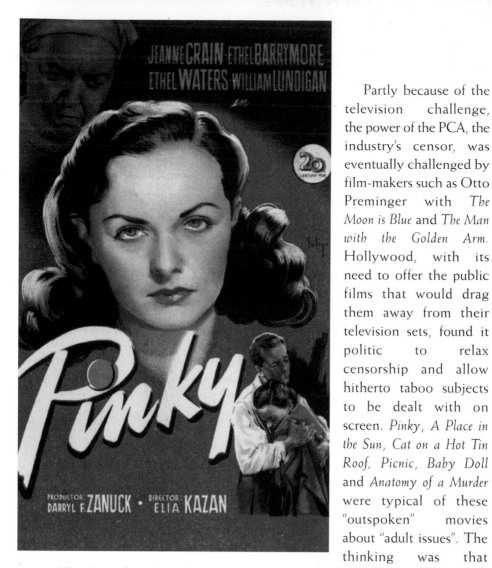

ABOVE *The subject of racial prejudice was tentatively dealt with in Elia Kazan's* Pinky.

Because the studios no longer had the incentive to make 50 or 60 movies a year to service their own movie-houses, long-term contract stars, directors, writers and other workers were gradually released. The numbers of movies produced by the majors decreased dramatically.

ABOVE *Otto Preminger's* Anatomy of a Murder (1959) *dealt with sexual matters in a way that would have had 1930s censors up in arms and demanding cuts.*

Partly because of the television challenge, the power of the PCA, the industry's censor, was eventually challenged by film-makers such as Otto Preminger with *The Moon is Blue* and *The Man with the Golden Arm.* Hollywood, with its need to offer the public films that would drag them away from their television sets, found it politic to relax censorship and allow hitherto taboo subjects to be dealt with on screen. *Pinky, A Place in the Sun, Cat on a Hot Tin Roof, Picnic, Baby Doll* and *Anatomy of a Murder* were typical of these "outspoken" movies about "adult issues". The thinking was that television was serving up anodyne fare such as *I Love Lucy,* so let's offer the public more adult material that

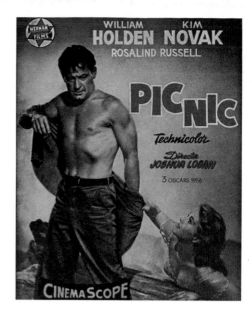

ABOVE *William Holden and Kim Novak starred in* Picnic (1955), *considered to be quite steamy in its time.*

television, in its pursuit of the family audience, could not compete with. Hollywood also discovered that most of its audience were between 16 and

BELOW *A Place in the Sun* (1951) *starring Elizabeth Taylor and Montgomery Clift was one of the movies that dealt with adult subjects with a new frankness.*

21

RIGHT *James Stewart and Barbara Bel Geddes in Hitchcock's* Vertigo, *which many people consider to be Hitch's finest achievement.*

25 years old, so movies deemed to appeal to this young audience were rapidly produced: *Rebel Without a Cause, The Wild One* and *Rock Around the Clock* were three such movies. The mass audience for movies had fragmented and Hollywood could no longer depend on income from movie-goers who regularly went to the cinema two or three times a week.

The 1950s was also the decade of pneumatic blondes, fantasy women created by men to pander to male chauvinism: Marilyn Monroe, Jayne Mansfield, Kim Novak, Diana Dors and Mamie Van Doren. Simultaneously new directors such as Sidney Lumet, John Frankenheimer and Martin Ritt learnt their craft in television studios and then transferred to the big screen. Alfred Hitchcock made some of his best films around this time, including *Rear Window, Vertigo, North by Northwest* and *Psycho*. Elia Kazan directed *On the Waterfront* and John Ford *The Searchers*. Alexander Mackendrick, after his successes with Ealing comedies such as *The Ladykillers* and *The Maggie*, went to Hollywood and made the classic *Sweet Smell of Success*. Declining audiences meant that Hollywood could not afford to take many chances on what it considered to be uncommercial material or unproven writers and directors but, despite

this lack of risk-taking, some good movies continued to be made in America.

However, it was with technological innovation that Hollywood principally gambled in its attempts to win back mass audiences: CinemaScope, VistaVision, 3-D, Todd-AO, Cinerama and other formats. Between the years 1954 and

1956 audience figures did show some increase compared to the preceding years, but the attractions of wide-screen and three-dimensional effects were short-lived and audience figures began to "dive" once again. In the USA, many people had fled the inner cities for the safety of the suburbs and were reluctant to venture back into the city in the evening to

23

OPPOSITE *Marilyn Monroe obliges a cop fan with her autograph.*

ABOVE *Alexander Mackendrick directed the most famous of all Ealing comedies,* The Ladykillers. *Mackendrick brought a misanthropic tone to the cosy world of Ealing comedy.*

ABOVE *20th Century Fox used CinemaScope to attract movie-goers back into the cinemas.*

ABOVE AND ABOVE RIGHT *Cinerama was a curved-screen alternative to CinemaScope, but few feature films were ever shot using this process.*

see a movie when they had the television on tap in their front room. It would take time for the suburban shopping mall movie-houses and multiplexes to catch up with this sociological phenomenon.

In the late 1950s and early 60s, French cinema gained new impetus with the *Nouvelle Vague* (New Wave) movement, led by directors such as François Truffaut, Jean-Luc Godard, Claude Chabrol, Louis Malle and Eric Rohmer. Ingmar Bergman directed a series of outstanding films in Sweden, including *The Seventh Seal* and *Wild Strawberries*. The international success of this "art cinema" testified to the fact that mass audiences were turning away from mainstream pictures, except in the case of epics such as MGM's remake of *Ben-Hur* and De Mille's remake of his own *The Ten Commandments*. Italy had led the way after the war in establishing this "art" market with the Neo-realist school of directors, pre-eminent of whom were Vittorio De Sica and Roberto Rossellini. Now, in the mid- to late 50s, a new generation of Italian directors was coming to the fore, including Michelangelo Antonioni (*L'Avventura*) and Federico Fellini (*La Dolce Vita, La Strada*). After a decade of making *Carry On* and *Doctor* movies, Ealing comedies and endless war movies, something stirred in British cinema and pictures such as *Room at the Top, A Taste of Honey, This Sporting Life, Saturday Night and Sunday Morning* and *Billy Liar* helped to extend the range of British films. Japanese cinema was also making a world impact, principally through Akira Kurosawa's films *Seven Samurai* and *Rashomon*. Eastern European cinema, particularly the Polish, Hungarian and Czechoslovakian industries, provided an outlet for covert social criticism, and directors such as Andrzej Wajda and Milos Forman became familiar names on the art-house circuit.

ABOVE *The war fable* Les Carabiniers (1963), *directed by Jean-Luc Godard, represented the Nouvelle Vague (New Wave) movement in French cinema.*

THE RISE OF THE AGENT AND THE PACKAGE DEAL

The butt of many a comedian's jokes, the agent, suddenly came to the fore in the power struggle in Hollywood. When the old studio system broke up, more and more films were made by independent producers who, however, had to make deals with the studios over distribution and, frequently, finance. The agents were ready to fill the vacuum that the demise of the studios as movie-making factories had left. Top agents, such as MCA and William Morris, could approach a studio with a

BELOW *New power-brokers Marlon Brando and Paul Newman confer. Major stars like these could now call the shots in new Hollywood.*

25

LEFT *Steve McQueen performs his own stunts in* The Great Escape, *something that would never have been allowed in old Hollywood.*

a package could ensure that a project would actually get off the ground.

The 60s, however, were not good years for Hollywood – at least until very late in the decade, when "youth" films such as *Easy Rider* and *The Graduate* emerged. Gone were the days of family pictures and the Louis B. Mayer ethos of "beautiful people in beautiful stories". Hollywood was now willing to make money from anything; and if youthful rebellion, after the heady days of 1968, was the fashion, then the new moguls were only too anxious to put youthful rebellion on screen.

In the 70s, a new generation of American directors arrived. Men such as Steven Spielberg, Martin Scorsese, Francis Coppola, Brian De Palma and George Lucas were steeped in Hollywood myths, and very often looked back to "old Hollywood" for their inspiration. Spielberg, for example, "raided" Disney films for *Close Encounters of the Third Kind* and *E.T.*, whilst Scorsese reinvented the MGM musical with *New York, New*

package deal that would consist of a screenplay by a well-known writer, a major star or two, an executive producer and a director – all of them under contract to the agency. The agents became the power-brokers of Hollywood. And although much was written about the end of the star system, a few major stars had more power than ever before. In the 1960s and 70s Barbra Streisand, Robert Redford, Jane Fonda, Marlon Brando, Dustin Hoffman, Steve McQueen, Paul Newman and others wielded immense power: their participation in

RIGHT *Steven Spielberg directed the block-buster* Jaws *(1975), which showed the new moguls that they could trust young directors with big-budget features.*

The terrifying motion picture from the terrifying No.1 best seller.

JAWS

ROY SCHEIDER · ROBERT SHAW · RICHARD DREYFUSS

JAWS

Co-starring LORRAINE GARY · MURRAY HAMILTON · A ZANUCK/BROWN PRODUCTION · Screenplay by PETER BENCHLEY and CARL GOTTLIEB
Based on the novel by PETER BENCHLEY · Music by JOHN WILLIAMS · Directed by STEVEN SPIELBERG · Produced by RICHARD D. ZANUCK and
DAVID BROWN · A UNIVERSAL PICTURE · TECHNICOLOR® PANAVISION® · [PG] PARENTAL GUIDANCE SUGGESTED · ORIGINAL SOUNDTRACK AVAILABLE ON MCA RECORDS AND TA
...MAY BE TOO INTENSE FOR YOUNGER CHILDREN

LEFT *Steven Spielberg directed new star Harrison Ford in* Raiders of the Lost Ark (1981), *a rousing adventure movie that paid tribute to the old Saturday morning cinema serials.*

York and remade John Ford's *The Searchers* in *Taxi Driver*. These "movie brats" were not only brilliant film-makers. They also knew how to make movies that would become all-time box-office winners, such as *Jaws, Star Wars* and *Raiders of the Lost Ark*. Audience figures would never return to their 1946 peak, but mega-hits in the cinema could make more money than ever before for their makers, including directors and stars who were usually on a percentage of the box-office revenues.

One feature of the 70s was the emergence of "new" national cinemas. Films that were both entertaining and important started to emerge from countries as diverse as the Sudan and Argentina. One of the strongest was the Australian cinema, led by *Picnic at Hanging Rock, Mad Max* and *My Brilliant Career*. Australian directors

RIGHT *The success of the first* Rambo *movie (1982) generated two sequels (1985, 1988) starring Sylvester Stallone, who rapidly became a power-broker in the industry.*

Peter Weir, Bruce Beresford and Fred Schepisi went on to direct movies in America. The German cinema experienced something of a reawakening with the emergence of directors such as Rainer Werner Fassbinder, Hans Werner Herzog and Wim Wenders. However, the British cinema was experiencing difficulty in maintaining a separate identity from the American industry, a situation that the French have never faced because they believe in an indigenous cinema and prove that by producing, on average, six times as many home-grown movies as the British do.

Cinema had become truly international by the 70s and 80s with directors such as Italy's Bernardo Bertolucci, France's Louis Malle and Germany's Wim Wenders making films in their native countries, Hollywood and elsewhere. The art film circuit was established, and if a film failed to find a wide release in the cinema, it could always get showings on some of the many television channels that were sprouting up in every country.

Video, and the fact that VCRs became part of almost every household, was the next challenge to cinema, but this time the businessmen behind the movie industry harnessed the new technology and turned it to their profit. For every one customer who sees a movie in the cinema, 12 now see it on video or DVD. In addition, the spread of cable and satellite television has added a new market for new and not-so-new films. Customers pay monthly premiums to watch new and old movies on channels dedicated to round-the-clock transmission of films. Or you can watch a new movie via pay-per-view. New movie productions are very often financed by cable companies such as HBO in America, or by television channels in Britain. But Hollywood in the 80s generally played it safe with winning formulas repeated ad nauseam, spawning endless sequels, and even "prequels". After all, just how many *Airplane!*, *Rocky* and *Halloween* sequels can the public accept?

27

COMPUTER TECHNOLOGY AND ANIMATION

No one can say with any certainty what the future holds for cinema. The accepted wisdom in Hollywood today is that "no one knows anything", meaning it is all a gamble because nobody can gauge public taste or how the industry will develop.

The importance of computerized technology to our society in general cannot be exaggerated. And the movie-making business has been and will continue to be transformed by that technology's ability to take over from humans some of the traditional skills associated with film-making. For example, when we think of the special effects created by specialists like Ray Harryhausen in the 1950s, 60s and 70s for movies such as *Jason and the Argonauts*, *One Million Years BC* and *The Golden Voyage of Sinbad*, the word "creaky" comes to mind. Compare

ABOVE Gladiator *employed state-of-the-art computer-generated special effects to flesh out its revenge story set in ancient Rome.*

those effects with the computer-generated effects of the *Jurassic Park* movies, the most recent *Star Wars* movies or *Gladiator*, and it can be seen how cinema technology is harnessing the advances in computer graphics to startling effect.

However, the "special effects" movies of the last 25 years, dating from 1977 when the first *Star Wars* was released with a resultant box-office harvest that has shaped Hollywood thinking ever since, seldom match their technical excellence with artistic worth. If we make a direct comparison of the Roman epics *Spartacus* (1960) and *Gladiator* (2000), is the latter with its computer-generated effects in the battle and gladitorial arena scenes in the same artistic league as the Kubrick-directed *Spartacus*, one of the few Hollywood epics that is not a no-brainer? *Spartacus* has a literate script by Dalton Trumbo, Kubrick's eye for

visual impact and is about more than just war and violence. The overrated *Gladiator* is basically a revenge western transcribed to Roman times, it isn't about anything very much, is directed by Ridley Scott and, for all its computer wizardy, fails to rise above the pedestrian. The point is that the technical advances of computerized graphics do not guarantee overall excellence – indeed, they very often guarantee the opposite because the special effects become the movie.

Two of the biggest box-office successes of recent years further illustrate this point: *Independence Day* (1996) and *Titanic* (1997). *Independence Day* made megabucks, but it is a spectacularly bad movie, inferior to many of the alien invasion movies of the 1950s (such as *The Day The Earth*

ABOVE The Day the Earth Stood Still *seemed in the forefront of cinematic special effects when it was released in the 1950s.*

ABOVE *The* Star Wars *movies ushered in a new era of special effects in Hollywood movies.*

Stood Still and *Invaders from Mars*) despite all the Oscar-winning special effects that were largely generated by computers. The script is laughable, the mock heroics of the Clinton-like president figure wholly implausible and the term "no-brainer" might well have been coined for this flick. They hardly come dumber than *Independence Day*, but *Titanic* certainly runs it close. Directed by James Cameron, and with the sinking of the Titanic spectacularly represented by state-of-the-art special effects, the movie itself is sunk by its third-rate "television special" script, its mawkishness, its stereotyped characterization and hackneyed storylines. It is almost as though the film-makers, having decided to film the Titanic disaster as

realistically and viscerally as possible, forgot the essential element of creating an adult and credible screenplay and decided just to go with what they had: a script that would not even pass muster for a television pilot.

Thus, computer-generated special effects cannot replace the need for scripts that escape banality or direction that is not merely at the service of the special-effects technicians. Not so long ago, there was industry talk about replacing actors such as Schwarzenegger and Stallone with their computer-generated "doubles". In other words, Arnie and Sly would not even have to be in one of their movies for there to be a Schwarzenegger or Stallone movie; the computer would do it for them. In those particular cases, perhaps the loss might not be that huge, but when stars can be replaced

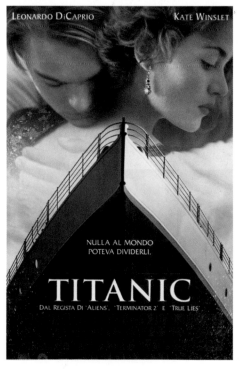

ABOVE *Titanic (1997) was a triumph of contemporary special effects, but lacked conviction in terms of story and characters.*

at will by their computerized doubles, then the industry needs to take a step back and consider what direction it is heading.

Another major technological advance of recent years has been in the field of animation, which is intimately linked with computerization. However, the end-products in animated films have been more encouraging. *Toy Story* and *Toy Story 2* have been much admired by people of all tastes and ages because the scripts are witty and intelligent, the graphics inventive and appealing, and the animation is at the service of the story. Other notable animated films of some worth have been *A Bug's Life*, *Antz*, *Stuart Little*, *Chicken Run* and *Shrek*. Disney have moved with the times with *The Lion King*, which took $220 million at the American box office and became the Disney Corporation's all-time biggest grosser. *Aladdin* and *Beauty and the Beast* also made huge profits,

although they were seen as more traditional Disney fare. There has always been a large market for adult strip-cartoon comics, and contemporary animated movies are reaching that market, as television animated series such as *The Simpsons*

and *South Park* have also done, the latter series having been turned into a successful feature film.

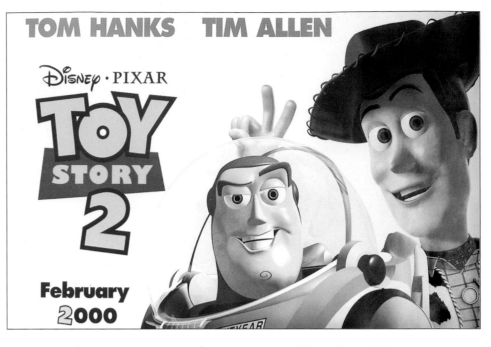

ABOVE *The producers of the Toy Story series lavished care on the quality of the scripts as well as the special effects.*

THE FUTURE

The advances in cinematic technology have been so rapid in the last decade or so that it would be a brave person who forecasts future developments in not only how movies are made but also how they are seen by the mass audience. However, I think we can be certain that

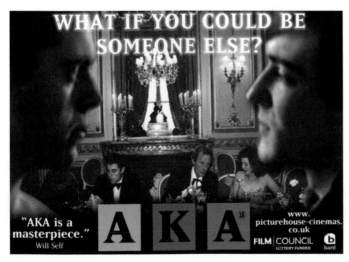

LEFT *AKA told its story on a screen that was split into three sections.*

"interactive cinema" may evolve at some future date, similar to so-called interactive television in that the viewer, in theory at least, can intervene and shape the spectacle he or she is watching. In other words, Aldous Huxley's "feelies" from *Brave New World* may be just around the technological corner. We may all sit in our cinema seats and press the appropriate button to add special effects such as smells, sounds or visual motifs to the movie we are watching.

Perhaps one day we will be able to alter storylines or movie endings to suit our own particular needs. Although there is no sign that cinema-going audiences are about to decline dramatically, there is always the possibility that people will retreat into their own homes to watch their movies, as more and more choice and control are handed over, in theory at least, to the customer.

Movies are now being shot on digital cameras, which reduces costs. It may be that this will be the path that independent film-makers in particular will have to follow. It is now possible for directors to shoot their films in one continuous take on digital cameras: no editing required – just an immense amount of pre-shooting rehearsal. Split-screen movies such as *AKA* (2002) may also have a future.

With the inevitable continuing spread of cable and satellite television and the emergence of top-quality DVD versions of movies (surely the days of videos are numbered), it is impossible to state categorically that cinema as we have known it will survive. The Hollywood film industry and its ownership change hands so rapidly nowadays, it is difficult to keep up with the latest deals and power-broking. Twenty-odd years ago, huge electronics firms such as Sony realized that they needed to control the production of movies to back the sales of their hardware.

When Sony subsequently bought Columbia, Harry Cohn, the long-time head of the studio and legendary movieland monster, must have been whizzing around in his grave. In a similar move, Rupert Murdoch's News International bought the 20th Century Fox studios to expand their control over different branches of the mass communication business. The old movies moguls such as Mayer and Zukor may have been tyrants and philistines at heart, but they could occasionally, given a nudge or two, recognize talent and they were at least involved in the day-to-day business of making movies. Contemporary owners of the major film production companies are generally not primarily movie people and seem much more

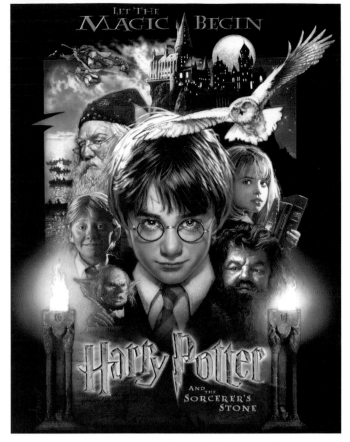

RIGHT The Harry Potter movies depend largely on the effectiveness of their computer-generated effects.

remote from the business of making pictures. An accusation made about contemporary Hollywood is that the accountants and the bankers are in charge and that explains why so many American films are the purest dross.

But it has really always been like this. There has always been a struggle between the people who want to make worthwhile movies and the entrepreneurs who just want to make millions.

There are not many producers around who would rather make *Citizen Kane* than a gross-out comedy such as *There's Something About Mary*. What will survive without doubt are movies themselves, however we choose to view them. But it is the fervent hope of this writer, and many others, I suspect, that people will continue to come together in movie houses to share the anticipation as the opening credits and the musical score jointly tell us that we are about to participate in that unique entertainment

LEFT Shrek had a witty script and terrific special effects, and took the animated film to new heights.

experience: the cinema. If the number of people actually going to cinemas shrinks significantly, then something irreplaceable will have gone from the business. The cinema-going experience is an important part of our communal culture.

However, too often cinema-going nowadays is not altogether a pleasurable experience – and for reasons not connected with the quality of the movies on offer. Cinemas now make as much money from their sales of grazing junk food as they do from ticket sales; the pervasive smells of hot dogs and popcorn, the rustling of sweetie bags, the crunching of crisps, not to mention talking, boorish behaviour and the ringing of mobile phones, threaten to make attendance at many local cinemas something of a trial. But when the movie is enthralling, when our minds and emotions are involved, and the audience shares that with you, then the cinema-going experience is like no other. Long may movie houses continue to prosper.

31

THE DIRECTORS

ORSON WELLES stated that movie directing was the most overrated profession in the world. In many ways, he was right. Some film directors are hacks who may have a certain level of technical know-how and the ability to command a film crew but who bring little else to the party. In some cases, a film's worth has little to do with the director. But other directors seem capable of producing images that mesmerize audiences. In this section we discuss the theory of "authorship". Whether or not the director can ever be seen as the "author" of a film, it is clear that some directors are a genuinely creative influence.

LEFT *Director Michael Curtiz with Errol Flynn and Olivia De Havilland, lighting cameraman, camera operator, sound recordist and make-up specialists shooting a scene for* Dodge City *(1939).*

INTRODUCTION

Movie-making is unavoidably and unarguably a collaborative exercise. In the very early days of Hollywood, it soon became apparent to the moneymen that an assembly-line form of production was the only economic way to meet the demands of making enough product to satisfy the weekly demands of the cinemas they themselves owned. Basically, those guys approached the business of turning out movies like Henry Ford did with motor cars. Never mind the quality; count the numbers. They recognized that there were several key personnel in this process, however – the directors, the cameramen, even the occasional writer, and perhaps the principal players. Loath as they were to allow these employees to feel themselves more important than the producers, the early moguls had to concede their central role in the movie-making process, and helped to build up their reputations as key selling points in the marketing of movies.

In those days, most movies were churned out one after the other on the stages and back lots of the studios. In the silent era, several movies would be

Director Alfred Hitchcock and star Bruce Dern sit and talk in a break from shooting Family Plot *(1976).*

ABOVE Singin' in the Rain *represents the assembly-line methods of early Hollywood.*

filming on different parts of the same vast stages. Think of the scene in *Singin' in the Rain* when Gene Kelly as Don Lockwood, silent-screen star, reports for the first day of shooting on his new swashbuckler. As he walks towards the stage where his movie is to be shot, he passes various westerns and jungle adventures already in the process of being filmed. His partner, played by Donald O'Connor, asks him what this movie he is going to start is about and when Kelly/Lockwood tells him, O'Connor/Cosmo remarks that he doesn't know why the studio bothers to make a new movie when they could release an old Don Lockwood movie under a new title. The implication is that no one would really notice – when you've seen one movie, you've seen them all. It is a humorous comment on the assembly-line form of production that was dominant in early Hollywood.

With the advent of sound pictures, movies could not be shot so close to one another, but the principle of assembly-line production remained the same. The battle in Hollywood has always been between the producers and investors on the one hand, and the "artists", the creative people on the other, whether they be directors, actors, cameramen, set designers, costume designers or composers of soundtracks. Too often,

crass commercialism has won out and the quality of the movies has suffered, but occasionally, despite the best efforts of philistine producers, something worthwhile gets made.

So who are the really key movie-makers, given that is a technological art and that the production process is so complicated and multifarious? Is the analogy with motor car manufacture relevant? After all, who makes a car? The original designer? The engineers? The mechanics who

ABOVE *Laurence Olivier directed and starred in the 1948 movie version of* Hamlet.

put it together? The engine-builders? A presiding genius? The fact is that they all contribute, but some contributors are more important than others and are the key players in the process. Film directors can legitimately claim to be key players in the film-making process, but their claims are not always justified, by any means. Some absurd claims have been made for individual film directors (such as Jerry Lewis, for example, or some Hollywood hack like Budd Boetticher), but such absurdities do not mean that some directors can be classed as the authors of the films they make. In this section of the book, we will look at the role of the director and some of the directors who have claims to be the major creative hands in the making of "their" movies.

MOVIE AUTHORSHIP

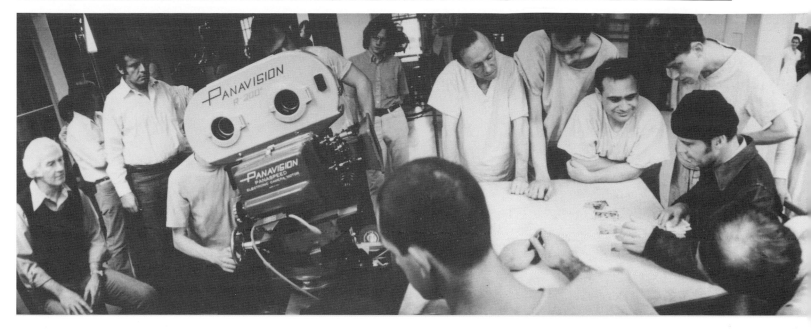

When we read a novel, we know who the author is. There are all sorts of arguments about authorship in literature. Post-structuralist theory has focused attention on the need to recognize the dependence of individual texts on other similar texts and suggested that it is not just the voice of the author that gives the text its meaning. The status of the author as the sole creator of the text and of any meaning it might contain has been put into serious question. Post-structuralists argue that we can ascribe any meaning to any text and should abandon the search for the meaning supposedly intended by an author.

Then, as the making of a movie is clearly a much more collaborative effort than the writing of a novel, is there any point in discussing the "authorship" of a movie? And if there is a point, who is this author? The screenwriter? Possibly the actors (some movie-goers still think the actors make up the lines as they go along)? The producer? The director? Perhaps even the film studio itself? Can we ever claim that there is one overall author of a finished commercial film?

The French movie critics in the 1940s and 50s were in no doubt. They looked at the commercial products of the Hollywood studios in particular and decided that the real authors of the movies they (the critics) liked were the directors of the films. They even went as far as to make a ranking list of directors who qualified for "auteur" status. A director was either one of these favoured with the accolade of "auteur" or he was a studio hack. There was no middle ground.

An "auteur" was a director who could claim to be the author of "his" films by creating a personal vision of the world within the film text. According to the auteur theory, these directors used the conventional elements of Hollywood film-making – the generic forms of the western or melodrama, the star system, the general mode of production, the conventional means of signifying meaning – to project an individual view of the world, whether it be a covert criticism of American society or some personal obsession.

Directors such as Alfred Hitchcock and Howard Hawks were cited as two of the "genius" directors who used conventional formats

(Hitchcock with his thrillers, Hawks across a whole range of genres – westerns, screwball comedy, actioners, science fiction, musicals) to pursue their particular themes and obsessions. Suddenly, even relatively unknown Hollywood directors were elevated to auteur status. Little did "B" picture directors such as Joseph H. Lewis and Budd Boetticher realize when they were making cheaply produced gangster pictures and

35

ABOVE *A movie such as* The Quiet Man (1952) *would be seen as essential to Ford's canon, the product of his own personal vision.*

ABOVE *Martin Ritt gives direction to Sally Field while filming* Norma Rae (1979).

westerns respectively that they would one day be feted by European critics as artists with a coherent philosophy of life embedded in their movies.

Younger British critics in the early 1960s took up the auteur theory, mainly in the pages of *Movie* magazine, and discovered their own heroes. Indeed, the first edition of *Movie* had definitive lists of "great", "excellent", "talented" and merely "competent" directors. To qualify for the top rankings, a director had to have a coherent vision that informed most of the movies he made. Thus, not only Hitchcock and Hawks qualified, but also Fritz Lang, Otto Preminger, Orson Welles, John Ford, Vincente Minnelli, Nicholas Ray and numerous others. Most of these directors were surprised when such critics pointed out to them that a coherent vision of the world shone through their films.

Undoubtedly directors are key figures in the process of making movies, but how many can truly be counted as the major artistic influence? It is a mistake to imagine that most films "belong" to a director, especially when the assembly-line mode of production that operated in Hollywood is considered. In old Hollywood, more often than not, a director would have little or no control over script and casting. For

example, Orson Welles was in South America trying to set up his next movie when RKO edited his second movie, *The Magnificent Ambersons*, in such a way as to produce the last few minutes of the movie that supplied a clichéd happy ending that was a betrayal of the dark perspective of Welles's vision. Directors were finally employees of the studios, and producers were there to make sure they did what the studio required.

However, there were some free spirits who did manage to use the system to make the films they wanted to make. Orson Welles is the outstanding example of a talented director who, after having made two brilliant movies, was sidelined by Hollywood because he was too much of an individualist. Hitchcock, on the other hand, won for himself a great deal of freedom by becoming the producer of his own movies and working out a deal over distribution with various major studios. A director had much more control over how he made "his" film when he had some economic involvement in the production; otherwise the studios who were putting up the money could largely dictate to him. In this situation, for a director who wanted to "say something" in movies, it was a matter of imposing some personal angle or trait where he could. However, there were some directors (John Ford, Howard Hawks, Vincente Minnelli, for example) who had the confidence of the studios and producers and were given their head to a certain extent

because they delivered the product in a form that was not only artistically satisfying but also made big bucks for the studio at the box office.

Since the break-up of the Hollywood studio system, numerous film-makers have won themselves much greater freedom over how they make their films. The packaging of a movie project (a script, a bevy of stars, a director, producer and an independent company) is done by agents who then deal with the studios who may act merely as distributors or bankers. Directors such as Steven Spielberg, George Lucas, James Cameron, the Coen Brothers and Woody Allen have far greater artistic control over their movies than those who worked under the old system.

However, that kind of freedom is not always productive because a director can be just as self-indulgent and tedious as writers can. Someone should have perhaps laid a restraining hand on Fellini, for example, before he turned out indulgent tosh like *Juliet of the Spirits*. The studio system was undoubtedly stifling to many talents, but the fact is that it also trained directors to work within certain disciplines; work of a surprisingly high quality was often produced in a business dedicated to making money.

ABOVE *British director Nicolas Roeg jokes with Tony Curtis and Michael Emil during the shooting of* Insignificance (1985).

"OLD HOLLYWOOD" GREATS

ALFRED HITCHCOCK
(1899–1980)

Of all the Hollywood directors that the French critics "rediscovered" in the 1950s, Alfred Hitchcock was the auteur who received the most attention and praise. His forte was the suspense thriller and he rarely changed the formula, but he used the genre, consciously and often unconsciously, to work through his own fears and obsessions. However, his first responsibility, as he saw it, was to make the audience squirm. He was a master of audience manipulation, presenting our fears, lusts, nightmares and weaknesses in the movies he directed; but in the process he revealed more about himself than he thought he was doing.

Born in Leytonstone, London, in 1899, Hitchcock had a lonely and repressed childhood, which left him with emotional scars that he spent the rest of his life exposing on screen. He also had a Catholic upbringing, which left him with a fear of authority, a sense of guilt — especially about sex — and the expectation of punishment. All these obsessions regularly surface in his movies. His obesity also gave him a complex about his unattractiveness to women. He usually cast very personable actors in the leading roles in his movies (Cary Grant, James Stewart, Gregory Peck) and put cool blondes opposite them; these glamorous women, however, would be subject to screen humiliation and sometimes murder. Joan Fontaine was the subject of Cary Grant's murderous intentions in *Suspicion* (the studio

insisted that Grant be cleared of suspicion at the end of the movie because it might have damaged his star image), Grant was beastly to Ingrid Bergman in *Notorious*, Ray Milland tried to murder Grace Kelly in *Dial M for Murder*, Kim Novak was thrown off a high tower (twice) in *Vertigo*, Janet Leigh was slaughtered in a shower in *Psycho*, Tippi Hedren was attacked by birds in *The Birds* and variously humiliated by Sean Connery in *Marnie*, and various women were raped and murdered in *Frenzy*.

ABOVE *Psycho and Hitchcock were attacked as depraved when the film was first released, but it has since been re-evaluated as one of the best-ever Hollywood movies.*

Hitchcock's favourite among his own movies was *Shadow of a Doubt*, starring Joseph Cotten as a charming uncle-figure who happened to have the distressing habit of bumping off widows for their money. No two fans would agree on Hitchcock's best films, but here is my choice: *Rebecca, Shadow of a Doubt, Notorious, Strangers on a Train, Vertigo, North by Northwest* and *Psycho. Blackmail, The Lodger, The Man Who Knew Too Much, Sabotage, The*

Thirty-Nine Steps and *The Lady Vanishes* are perhaps the best of his British output before he went to Hollywood. *Suspicion, Spellbound, I Confess, Dial M for Murder, The Wrong Man, The Birds* and *Marnie* all have outstanding Hitchcockian scenes in them. His last movies, *Torn Curtain, Topaz, Frenzy* and *Family Plot* represent the world of his dotage.

Whether consciously or not, Hitchcock challenged the audience to consider themselves as voyeurs. He knew that we are fascinated by the process of watching — and the cinema makes voyeurs of us all. He played on our fantasies and made us feel guilty about what they reveal about ourselves. He could manipulate us to feel anxiety for the "wrong people": for example, after Norman Bates has murdered Marion Crane (Janet Leigh) in the shower scene in *Psycho*, albeit dressed as his mother, we watch anxiously as he cleans up the blood, remembers the newspaper containing the money in the bedroom at the last moment, stuffs the dead body into the boot of Leigh's car and drives to the swamp. When the car stops halfway down in the swamp, we want it to continue to submerge even though it contains the murdered body. Hitchcock has successfully transferred our sympathy from the victim to the murderer, manipulating our emotions in a manner that leaves us feeling distinctly uncomfortable. He was at the very least a master cinematic storyteller, but there are perhaps depths of meaning to his films that go beyond the conventional thriller.

37

JOHN FORD (1895–1973)

John Ford consistently denied any serious artistic purpose in his work, and hooted with laughter at the idea of any consistent philosophy permeating the movies he directed. But critics have marked him down as one of the great originals of the Hollywood scene; some see him as a poet of the cinematic image, and certainly some of his films contain stunning visual images and dramatic power. However, there are unarguably distasteful elements to them (racism in their representation of Native Americans, extreme conservative values including glorifying militarism and a gung-ho American patriotism, mindless violence, crude slapstick humour and a prevalent sexism). He is best known for his westerns: *Stagecoach, Drums Along the Mohawk, My Darling Clementine, Fort Apache, She*

"Don't ever forget what I'm going to tell you. Actors are crap."
John Ford

Wore a Yellow Ribbon, Rio Grande, Wagonmaster, The Searchers and *The Man Who Shot Liberty Valance* are among his best known. His politics were a kind of maverick right-wing extremism, which may explain why he used stars with similar political beliefs, such as John Wayne and Ward Bond, so often in his movies.

John Ford's films generally deal with groups of men in situations where they have to show their courage and loyalty to one another. He could be extremely sentimental at times, especially in his "Oirish" movies such as *The Quiet Man* and *The Last Hurrah*. American Indians are portrayed as savages in almost all of the westerns until *The Searchers* (1956), but there is a belated attempt to redress the balance in the 1964 *Cheyenne Autumn*. At its best, Ford's work has a warmth and humanity about it (*The Grapes of Wrath, The Long Voyage Home, Young Mr Lincoln*); at its worst it celebrates a kind of mindless, brutal machismo (*They Were*

ABOVE *The Searchers (1956) is rated as one of the best westerns ever made and is a major opus of John Ford.*

Expendable, Donovan's Reef). Running through the body of his films is a romanticized militarism and a lament for an America that has vanished forever, a lawless frontier culture that was obliterated by the march of civilization and the law book.

BELOW *Henry Fonda as Abraham Lincoln in Ford's* Young Mr Lincoln, *a rather solemn biopic of the legendary American president.*

HOWARD HAWKS (1896–1977)

Hawks is a test case for the theory that certain directors have a consistent vision that shines through all the films they direct, because he was the archetypal journeyman director elevated to auteur status initially by the French critics and then later by supporters of the auteur theory. Born in Indiana, Hawks directed movies across a wide range of genres: actioners (*Barbary Coast, Only Angels Have Wings, To Have and Have Not, The Big Sky*), westerns (*Red River, Rio Bravo, El Dorado*), screwball comedies (*Twentieth Century, Bringing Up Baby, His Girl Friday*), gangsters (*Scarface*), private eye thrillers (*The Big Sleep*), science fiction (*The Thing*), musicals (*Gentlemen Prefer Blondes*) and epics (*Land of the Pharaohs*).

> " WHEN YOU FIND OUT A THING GOES PRETTY WELL, YOU MIGHT AS WELL DO IT AGAIN."
> *HOWARD HAWKS*

He is quoted as saying, "For me the best drama is one that deals with a man in danger," and that holds true for most of his movies. How much overall control he had over the content of his movies remains in doubt, however, and how much he deserves auteur status remains a matter of judgement. I think it is safe to say that his reputation has declined since the heady days when the French among others claimed him as a cinematic genius.

ABOVE *Howard Hawks directed Bogart in* The Big Sleep. *At one point he found the plot so complicated that he had to telephone writer Raymond Chandler to explain it; Chandler couldn't help out. The movie is more about style than narrative coherence, and macho cool rather than love between men and women.*

THE TALENTED JOURNEYMEN

FRANK CAPRA (1897–1991)

Many would claim that Capra belongs in the first rank of American directors for the body of "populist" films he made in the 1930s and 40s in which he celebrated the essential decency of the common man and the virtues of American democracy. Capra's populism consisted of his taking the side of the little guy against the battalions of big business and organized politics. A simplistic philosophy and wish-fulfilling happy endings are found in *Mr Deeds Goes to Town* (Gary Cooper inheriting wealth and going to New York to help poor farmers), *You Can't Take It with You, Mr Smith Goes to Washington* (James Stewart sorting out the political machine), *Meet John Doe* and *It's a Wonderful Life* in which Stewart again saves small-town America from perdition. As well as these movies, Capra directed Harlow in *Platinum Blonde*, Gable and Colbert in *It Happened One Night*, Ronald Colman in *Lost Horizon* and Tracy and Hepburn in *State of the Union*. His later films were entirely forgettable: *Riding High* and *Here Comes the Groom* with Crosby, and *A Hole in the Head* with Sinatra. *It's a Wonderful Life* is undoubtedly one of the favourite Hollywood movies for many people, and its sentimentality and whimsy are hard to resist.

ABOVE It's a Wonderful Life *(1946) is a perennial favourite, defying critical rigour.*

ABOVE *Frank Capra directs Bing Crosby on the set of* Here Comes the Groom *(1951).*

MICHAEL CURTIZ (1888–1962)

Curtiz was Hungarian by birth and had a substantial career in European films before he came to Hollywood to direct some of the most famous pictures of the 1930s and 40s. He directed Errol Flynn in *Captain Blood, The Charge of the Light Brigade, The Perfect Specimen, The Adventures of Robin Hood, The Private Lives of Elizabeth and Essex, Dodge City, Virginia City, The Sea Hawk* and *Sante Fe Trail*. He showed he had a feeling for romance and *film noir* in the classic *Casablanca* and *Mildred Pierce*. He directed Cagney in *Yankee Doodle Dandy*, Claude Rains in the *film noir The Unsuspected* and Elvis Presley in *King Creole*. He also made real turkeys

ABOVE *Director Michael Curtiz, on the ground, watches leading man Errol Flynn turn on the charm in the western* Dodge City. *Curtiz directed Flynn in nine movies.*

such as *The Egyptian, The Jazz Singer* (the 1953 version) and *The Vagabond King*. Primarily associated with Warner Brothers, Curtiz was the quintessential journeyman director, turning his directorial hand to most genres; however, very few critics, even the most obsessive of French auteurists, have made a case for Curtiz's "vision". Curtiz helped to give some of the movies he directed a certain visual style, but beyond that, he had little to contribute.

ABOVE *Cecil B. De Mille's 1956 version of* The Ten Commandments.

ABOVE *George Cukor directed Joan Crawford in this melodrama,* A Woman's Face *(1941).*

GEORGE CUKOR (1899–1983)

Cukor came to be known as a woman's director because of the sensitivity with which he handled top female stars and "women's pictures". He was also known for directing respectable screen adaptations of famous literary works such as *Little Women, David Copperfield, Romeo and Juliet* and *The Women.* Musicals included *A Star is Born, Les Girls* and *My Fair Lady.* Comedies were perhaps his forte: *The Philadelphia Story, Adam's Rib, Born Yesterday, The Marrying Kind* and *Pat and Mike.* He also directed Greta Garbo in *Camille,* Joan Crawford in *A Woman's Face,* Bette Davis in *The Actress* and Marilyn Monroe in *Let's Make Love.* Cukor's main talent may have consisted of his ability to adapt literary and theatrical influences to the cinema and to serve up middlebrow entertainment in various forms over a period of 40 years. He managed to survive as a gay man in "old Hollywood" without scandal breaking over his head.

WILLIAM WYLER (1902–81)

Wyler, of German origin, was known as a very hard taskmaster for actors. He took no nonsense from even the biggest stars such as Bette Davis, who was notoriously difficult in her heyday and whom he directed in *Jezebel, The Letter* and *The Little Foxes,* or Laurence Olivier, who in his youth displayed a disdain for Hollywood that did not sit well with the autocratic Wyler. To his credit, Olivier later paid tribute to Wyler's influence on him as a director and actor after he had directed him in *Wuthering Heights.* One of his most important movies was *The Best Years of Our Lives,* which examined the problems facing ex-GIs coming to terms with the post-war USA, and offered some liberal but simplistic solutions. Wyler was also entrusted with action pictures, notably *The Desperate Hours, The Big Country* and

ABOVE *Journeyman director Henry King (1888–1982) has his fans even when directing swashbucklers such as* Captain from Castile *with Tyrone Power.*

Ben-Hur. Charlton Heston, the star of *Ben-Hur,* is quoted as saying, "Doing a picture with Willie is like getting the works at a Turkish bath. You damn near drown, but you come out smelling like a rose." Melodramas directed by Wyler included *The Heiress, Carrie* and *The Children's Hour,* and he also directed Streisand in *Funny Girl.*

ABOVE *William Wyler directed the post-war drama* The Best Years of Our Lives *(1946), about the difficulties of ex-GIs and their families readjusting to peacetime.*

VINCENTE MINNELLI
(1903–86)

Minnelli was one of MGM's longest-serving directors. Indeed, in a career spanning 35 years, he made only three films out of 36 for studios other than MGM. This makes him an interesting test case as a director: as a resident studio director with some talent, how much control did he have over the movies he made?

Minnelli is best known for his musicals, but he has also acquired a reputation for the melodramas he directed in the 1950s. These include *The Cobweb*, *The Bad and the Beautiful*, *Some Came Running* and *Home from the Hill*. His best-known musicals are *Meet Me in St Louis*, *The Pirate*, *An American in Paris*, *The Band Wagon*, *Gigi* and *On a Clear Day You Can See Forever*. He is, in fact, known as the father of the modern movie musical and has other paternity claims as the father of Liza Minnelli, the product of his brief marriage to Judy Garland. His favourite film of the ones he directed himself was *Lust for*

LEFT *One of the most popular musicals Vincente Minnelli directed was* Gigi *(1958), adapted from a novella by Colette and a book by Alan Jay Lerner. The score was written by Frederick Loewe.*

Life in which Kirk Douglas played Van Gogh. Minnelli was revered by critics as a stylist and for his feeling for colour and design within the screen space. Yet he seldom or ever found his own projects to film, and never had final cutting rights over what he had shot. Indeed, some of his movies were partially reshot or completed by other directors (*An American in Paris*, *Gigi*, *The Seventh Sin*) and as one of MGM's most successful and highly-thought-of

directors, he was shunted from movie to movie without much time for reflection. Yet, despite all this, some critics still manage to discover a consistent vision of the world incorporated in his movies. If we accept that style is meaning, then Minnelli could be said to have a consistent philosophy in the movies he directed, but his supporters go beyond that to discover common thematic obsessions and narrative resolutions personal to the director. He certainly never thought of himself as the author of his movies and like other Hollywood stalwarts was very surprised when these claims were made on his behalf. He may not have been an intellectual director, but he "said" something through the application of his style.

BELOW *Minnelli directed one of the best movies about Hollywood,* The Bad and the Beautiful *(1952), which starred Kirk Douglas as a David Selznick-like producer.*

ABOVE *Fritz Lang, the German expressionist director of* Metropolis *(1927) found a new career in Hollywood. A western he directed with Marlene Dietrich,* Rancho Notorious *(1952), has become a cult movie.*

BILLY WILDER (1906–2002)

Another European expatriate of Austrian origin, Wilder specialized in rather sour comedy and noirish melodramas. He co-wrote, with Charles Brackett and then I.A.L. Diamond, many of the films he directed. As a writer, he collaborated on Garbo's *Ninotchka* and the Stanwyck–Cooper *Ball of Fire*. As a writer-director, his finest efforts were *Double Indemnity* (on which he collaborated with Raymond Chandler) and *Sunset Boulevard*. Other notable films include *Ace in the Hole*, *The Seven Year Itch*, *Some Like it Hot* and *The Apartment*. His later films became increasingly raucous and vulgar: *Irma La Douce*, *Kiss Me Stupid* and *Avanti!* Wilder was quoted as saying that the best direction is the one you don't see; certainly, he was no stylist and his main talent may have been as a writer and in his instinct for what worked on screen. He was clever enough to choose talented collaborators and when that collaboration worked, he was instrumental in making some of Hollywood's finest. But an auteur?

ABOVE Billy Wilder directed The Apartment, *which many people think superior fare to rather vulgar comedies such as* Some Like it Hot, The Fortune Cookie *and* Kiss Me Stupid.

Certainly not. He himself dismissed the auteur theory as intellectualizing nonsense. However, Wilder was involved in making some of Hollywood's best movies, which reinforces the argument that the overwhelming majority of movies are a genuinely collaborative effort.

GEORGE STEVENS (1904–75)

Stevens's best film as a director is probably *Shane*, the classic western, and yet he was not a western specialist. He made a name in the 1930s directing Hepburn in *Alice Adams* and again in *Woman of the Year*. His films tended towards the sentimental and the romantic, for example, *I Remember Mama* and *A Place in the Sun*. He directed Dean, Taylor and Hudson in the Texan epic *Giant* and was also responsible for *The Greatest Story Ever Told*. During World War II, he directed some of the most impressive footage of the conflict and the liberation of the Nazi concentration camps. Undoubtedly, Stevens had a sure instinct for manipulating the emotions of the cinema audience: *Shane* and *A Place in the Sun* are guaranteed to produce tears. It is, however, perhaps that talent to manipulate that defines his limitations as a director. He is an interesting test case for a Hollywood director: auteur or talented hack?

ABOVE George Stevens directed Liz Taylor and Rock Hudson in the Texan epic Giant *(1956). The movie is best known as James Dean's last movie before his death in a car accident in 1955.*

JOHN HUSTON (1906–87)

A talented director or a lucky son of a famous father who happened to get involved with some decent movies? Opinions divide over John Huston largely because there is little discernible pattern to his work. He himself is quoted as saying, "I fail to see any continuity in my work from picture to picture." One can see a pattern of a rather bogus male camaderie and machismo, however. There is a

direct some of the best of Hollywood movies: *The Maltese Falcon, The Treasure of the Sierra Madre, The Asphalt Jungle, The Misfits* and *Wise Blood.* However, he also directed some of the worst: *Moulin Rouge, Moby Dick, The Barbarian and the Geisha, The Bible...In the Beginning* and *Escape to Victory.* The jury is still out on *Prizzi's Honour* and *The Dead.*

"WE CAN MAKE BAD PICTURES TOO. COSTS MORE BUT WE CAN MAKE 'EM."
JOHN HUSTON

Huston was certainly no stylist in the sense that Orson Welles was. He himself disclaimed any thematic continuity in his movies, so what exactly was his contribution to the movies he directed?

He was able, by all accounts, to bully a performance out of actors, had a fairly sure instinct for some of the projects he directed, and worked with able collaborators. That does not make him in any way the author of the movies he directed. As an actor in movies such as *The Bible...In the Beginning* and *Chinatown*, he tended to the "hammy" and in public interviews he came over as playing John Huston the legendary film director rather than emerging from behind that mask he wore. However, there is no doubting his staying power or his iconic status among old Hollywood directors. Undoubtedly, he was associated with some of the better movies Hollywood made in its heyday.

BELOW *Joseph L. Mankiewicz (1909–93) was an important and talented writer-director. All About Eve, about New York theatre people, is a much-admired movie.*

ABOVE *John Huston had a hit with the first film he directed,* The Maltese Falcon *starring Humphrey Bogart and Mary Astor.*

compelling portrait of Huston in Clint Eastwood's 1990 movie *White Hunter, Black Heart;* the movie centres around a Hollywood director shooting a movie in Africa that is clearly intended to be *The African Queen*, and the Huston-like character is obsessed with shooting big game resulting in the unnecessary death of an African servant. In the 1973 *The Way We Were,* the cowardly lefty Hollywood director (played by Patrick O'Neal) who caves into McCarthyite pressure is clearly based on Huston. Despite his personal and professional failings, Huston did

THE MAVERICKS

This section focuses on "maverick" directors who, for one reason or another, did not quite fit in with the Hollywood system, or who carved out for themselves a unique position within that system.

JOSEF VON STERNBERG (1894–1969)

Another Austrian expatriate director, Von Sternberg's career was closely associated with the films in which he directed Marlene Dietrich. Neither of their careers ever really recovered from their professional split, though Von Sternberg suffered more than the star he "created".

Von Sternberg was known as a stylist; indeed he is quoted as saying that he cared little for the stories of his films, only about how they were photographed and presented. That is just as well because movies such as *Shanghai Express*, *Morocco*, *Blonde Venus*, *The Scarlet Empress* and *The Devil is a Woman* teeter on the edge of being "high camp" rubbish and only the "look" of them saves them. Von Sternberg liked shooting through shutters and lattices, gauze and mists; he also decorated his sets elaborately to create a Hollywood concept of decadence. There is a campness about his most famous movies.

After his films with Dietrich, his career went into a downward spiral; he directed the unfinished *I Claudius* for Korda and then made very few films until his death in 1969. He once said, "The only way to succeed is to make people hate you. That way they remember you." It seems that people remembered Von Sternberg's autocratic ways only too well, because very few of them offered him a directing job in his declining years.

BELOW *Josef Von Sternberg directed Jane Russell in the strange, exotic melodrama* Macao *in 1952. Style was everything to Sternberg — much more important than story.*

ORSON WELLES (1915–85)

The enfant terrible of Hollywood in the 1940s, Welles first came to fame when he terrorized America with his documentary-style radio version of H.G. Wells's *The War of the Worlds*, convincing thousands of Americans that their country was being invaded by aliens. *Citizen Kane* (1941) then established his reputation as a director of movies; his story of a press baron, based on the life of William Randolph Hearst, was seen as innovatory in its use of deep-focus photography,

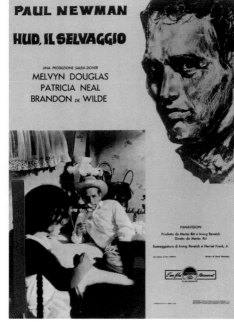

ABOVE *Always battling against lack of money, Orson Welles made several Shakespearian movies.* Othello *has its pluses and minuses – but at least it got made.*

ABOVE *Martin Ritt (1914–90) made this study of male bravado,* Hud, *in 1963. Other notable films he directed include* Edge of the City *(1956),* The Spy Who Came in from the Cold *(1965) and* Norma Rae *(1979).*

overlapping sound, expressionistic sets and creative montage sequences. How much of the credit for these innovations should go to cameraman Gregg Toland and co-writer Herman J. Mankiewicz is still a matter of controversy. Welles's second film for RKO, *The Magnificent Ambersons*, was badly mauled by the studio, which added a spurious happy ending. Thereafter, Welles's relationship with the studios declined, and he was more often seen as an actor in films made by others, such as *Jane Eyre, Prince of Foxes, The Third Man, The Black Rose, Moby Dick, The Long Hot Summer* and *The Roots of Heaven*. Some of the later films he directed have authentic Welles touches to them, notably *The Stranger, Macbeth, Othello, The Lady from Shanghai, Touch of Evil,*

> "EVERYONE DENIES I AM A GENIUS BUT NO ONE EVER CALLED ME THAT IN THE FIRST PLACE."
> *ORSON WELLES*

> "DIRECTING FILMS IS THE MOST OVER-RATED PROFESSION IN THE WORLD."
> *ORSON WELLES*

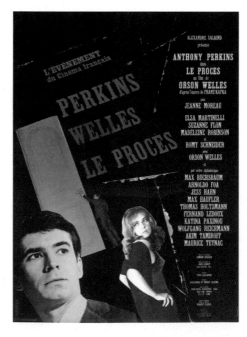

ABOVE *Orson Welles directed* The Trial *in 1962, a film adaptation of Kafka's famous novel. Shot in the old Gare D'Orsay station in Paris, it suffered somewhat from Welles's usual underbudgeting.*

The Trial, Chimes at Midnight and *The Immortal Story*. The usual adjective used about his later work is "flawed", but many of those flaws were caused by very low, even disappearing budgets. Welles said of himself, "I started at the top and worked down", and there is more than a grain of truth in that statement, including the implication that he may have brought many of his troubles upon his own head. However, *Kane* and *Ambersons* alone elevate him to the status of major director. Hollywood could not handle his maverick genius and he could not handle Hollywood.

NICHOLAS RAY (1911–79)

Ray became an icon for many European critics and film-makers – another figure, like Welles, identified

ABOVE *Nicholas Ray directed John Wayne and Robert Ryan in the tough war movie* The Flying Leathernecks *(1951).*

as a genius director partly destroyed by the studio system. His artistic background was with the left-wing Group Theatre, where he was a protégé of Elia Kazan. His first Hollywood film *They Live by Night* is probably his best; the story of the isolated and alienated young lovers (played by Farley Granger and Cathy O'Donnell) is given added impact by Ray's imaginative use of the screen space and his creative mise-en-scène. Ray clearly identified with the outsider and the young in American society, and this was again reflected in his direction of James Dean in *Rebel Without a Cause*. The institution of the family gets a rough ride in several of his films, notably in *They Live by Night, Rebel* and also in *Bigger Than Life*, where James Mason takes medical drugs and is transformed into an oppressive patriarch – his real self, the movie implies. Ray also made *In a Lonely Place*, a study of paranoia and violence

starring Humphrey Bogart as a Hollywood writer; this movie was perceived as being a comment on the paranoia engendered by the McCarthyite investigations into Hollywood in the late 40s and early 50s.

French critics in particular saw merits in later Ray films such as *Bitter Victory* and *Party Girl* that few other people could perceive, and they even found things to admire in two epics he

ABOVE *Nicholas Ray's* Rebel Without a Cause *made James Dean a screen icon for millions. It is the ultimate teen-angst movie.*

directed in the early 60s, *King of Kings* and *55 Days at Peking*. Wim Wenders, the German director, paid one last tribute when he made a film about Ray when the American was dying of cancer in 1979, *Lightning over Water*. This was a last defiant romantic gesture from a romantic director.

ELIA KAZAN (b. 1909)

Kazan, of Greek descent, worked in the 1930s as an actor with the left-wing Group Theatre in New York, but later he spectacularly re-nounced his radical past when he served as a friendly witness in front of the Congressional com-mittee investigating so-called communist infiltration into Hollywood in the 1940s and 50s. Kazan went so far as to "name names" of past Communist associates to the committee. His testimony

LEFT *Elia Kazan directed* Gentleman's Agreement *(1947), a movie about anti-semitism in the USA. It starred Gregory Peck as an investigative journalist, Dorothy McGuire and John Garfield.*

and also demonstrations inside and outside the auditorium where the Oscars ceremony was being held.

DOUGLAS SIRK (1900–87)

Of Danish origin, Sirk worked in the German Expressionist theatre of the 1920s before directing various European films and coming to Hollywood. His first major film was *Summer Storm* (1944), adapted from a Chekhov short story, then he made a series of comedies for Universal including *Has Anybody Seen My Gal?*, *Meet Me at the Fair* and *Take Me to Town*. However,

probably saved his own career, but at the expense of the careers of other Hollywood colleagues, who never forgave him.

Kazan's early films are far from personal: *A Tree Grows in Brooklyn*, *Gentleman's Agreement*, *The Sea of Grass* and *Pinky*. He described MGM, for whom he made *The Sea of Grass*, as an industrial compound run by business-men. His first personal project was *A Streetcar Named Desire* with Marlon Brando and Vivien Leigh and, after his testimony to the Congressional committee, he concentrated on making movies which, to varying degrees, seemed to justify the stand he had taken. *On the Waterfront* justified "snitching" on your friends when it showed Terry Malloy (Brando) turning stool-pigeon on his erstwhile gangster pals; the movie was also a huge success and gave Kazan carte blanche to tackle any film project he wanted to and have final cut rights over the movies he made. He went on to make *East of Eden*, *Baby Doll*, *A Face in the Crowd*, *Wild River*, *Splendor in the Grass* and *The Last Tycoon*. In between

he made two films which he adapted from his own novels, *America America* and *The Arrangement*. In these films he represents his family's coming to the USA and experiencing the joys and tribulations of American capitalism. Kazan's main talents were his undoubted ability to direct actors and the emotional intensity he brought to his movies. Controversially, in 1998 he was awarded an honorary Oscar, a gesture that brought much vocal criticism from survivors of the McCarthyite perse-cutions in Hollywood

RIGHT *Robert Rossen (1908–66) made unusual Hollywood movies such as* Lilith. *Other major films Rossen directed include* The Hustler *and* All the King's Men.

ABOVE *Douglas Sirk directed a series of melodramas for Universal-International in the 1950s and 60s.* Magnificent Obession, *starring Rock Hudson and Jane Wyman, was released in 1954.*

Sirk's reputation as an auteur – and he has numerous supporters as such – rests squarely on the melodramas he directed in the 1950s: *All I Desire, Magnificent Obsession, There's Always Tomorrow, All That Heaven Allows,*

Written on the Wind, The Tarnished Angels and *Imitation of Life.* Supporters of Sirk's claims to seriousness say that he used the excesses of the melodramatic genre to criticize the era of Eisenhower's America in all its materialism and conformity. Detractors of these claims say that you can read anything you like into these excessively sentimental pieces of schlock if you really want to find an excuse for liking them. However,

there is little doubt that Sirk used ironic and distancing devices in his direction to draw attention to the social points he wanted to make. His left-wing credentials endeared him to many film critics in Europe, but some feminist critics, although admitting his films were more than just examples of kitsch, pointed out that they did tend to reinforce patriarchal structures while appearing to attack them. Another aspect of Sirk's directing is his use of colour, camera angles and reflecting surfaces such as mirrors. His melodramas often employ a fast editing technique and the effect is almost like a strip cartoon of imagery. A good example of this is the opening pre-credits sequence to *Written on the Wind*: Robert Stack drives his red sports car at speed, he arrives at the family mansion, a concerned face appears at the window, he enters the mansion and climbs the staircase, the leaves blow into the hall, there is a gunshot. It is, in its own way, a brilliant use of editing technique to build tension and reach the melodramatic heights to which these movies aspire.

STANLEY KUBRICK (1928–99)

After two minor, low-budget films, Kubrick, who had been a photographer with *Life* magazine, made *The Killing* (1956), a semi-documentary crime thriller which brought him much attention. *Paths of Glory*, an anti-war movie set in World War 1 trenches with Kirk Douglas as a French officer defending three men wrongfully accused of cowardice, established his reputation as a major director. The epic *Spartacus* continued his association with Kirk Douglas, and is usually seen as one of the few intelligent epics.

Kubrick's desire to film challenging material led him to direct *Lolita* in 1962, and he used the movie to paint a picture of an America that was aimless and materialistic. His black

LEFT *Dr Strangelove* (1964) *is a hilarious satire on Cold War thinking and the American military. It still has much relevance today.*

OPPOSITE *Kubrick's* 2001: A Space Odyssey (1968) *is rated by many as by far the best of all space travel movies. It has its obscurities, but it remains a major work of this director.*

Kubrick insisted on independence as a producer-director and his films were always notable, though he has been criticized for being too interested in his sets and staging of events at the expense of the characters. Certainly, since *Paths of Glory*, there was a distancing of emotional involvement, but he remained a great talent throughout his career.

comedy *Dr Strangelove* remains a very funny comment on the nightmare of the dangers of nuclear warfare and *2001: A Space Odyssey* in 1968 took the space film into new dimensions. *A Clockwork Orange* was controversially violent and aroused a storm of protest (Kubrick later withdrew it from circulation), but *Barry Lyndon* was largely damned with the faint praise of being beautiful to look at but not much else. It is, however, one of the greatly underrated movies of the 1970s. *The Shining* again aroused protests because of its violence, particularly towards women. *Full Metal Jacket* was Kubrick's Vietnam movie, and it is certainly among the best of the crop of movies about that American nightmare. The movie he had just completed before his untimely death in 1999, *Eyes Wide Shut* (starring Tom Cruise and Nicole

Kidman), however, is sadly an unworthy last legacy of a director who can truly be said to have been a major talent in the art of film-making.

ABOVE *After the critical mauling* A Clockwork Orange *received on its release in* 1971, *Kubrick withdrew the movie from circulation for many years. Some critics see the movie as a major work, others as a kind of aberration from this endlessly inventive director.*

THE DIRECTORS OF NEW HOLLYWOOD

JOHN CASSAVETES (1929–89)

Cassavetes was never a hugely successful director, but he made the movies he wanted to in his own personal style. He was a successful Hollywood actor (in *Edge of the City* and *Virgin Island*) before he turned to directing, but it was his experimental film *Shadows* (1961) that established his reputation for risk-taking: actors' improvisation, hand-held cameras, disjointed narrative and a refusal to portray human relationships sentimentally. He is quoted as saying, "When I started making pictures, I wanted to make Frank Capra pictures. But I've never been able to make anything but these crazy tough pictures. You are what you are." "These crazy tough pictures" include *Faces* (1968), *Husbands* (1970), *A Woman Under the Influence* (1974), *The Killing of a Chinese Bookie* (1976), *Opening Night* (1977), *Gloria* (1980) and *Love Streams* (1984). Only *Gloria* achieved any substantial commercial success. His wife, Gena Rowlands, starred in most of his films and he himself also acted in some of them. Other favourite male actors he used were Peter Falk and Ben Gazzara, who were his personal friends. Almost all of the films Cassavetes directed have real flaws in them, but there is a rawness and honesty that distinguishes them sharply from the standard Hollywood product. Tragically, he died in 1989 at the age of 60.

> "I NEVER KNOW WHAT MY MOVIES ARE ABOUT UNTIL I FINISH THEM."
> *JOHN CASSAVETES*

STEVEN SPIELBERG (b. 1946)

Spielberg is the world's most famous and successful living film director. He makes movies for the mass market and is phenomenally successful at it. *Jaws*, *Close Encounters of the Third Kind*, *E.T.*, *Raiders of the Lost Ark*, *Indiana Jones and the Temple of Doom*, *Indiana Jones and the Last Crusade*, *Jurassic Park*, *Schindler's List* and *Saving Private Ryan* have made him a multi-millionaire and carved him a very powerful position within the American film industry. He is the most consistently successful of the "movie brats", that group of movie-obsessed young men who conquered Hollywood in the 1970s: George Lucas, Francis Coppola, Martin Scorsese, Brian De Palma, Peter Bogdanovich and Spielberg himself. He has garnered critical praise as well as commercial success.

Spielberg openly confesses his debt to Disney and the Saturday-morning serials, but his films are also in the tradition of Frank Capra populism – they are for the individual against bureaucracy and on the side the decent instincts of the ordinary people against the government that appears to act in their name. Witness the Richard Dreyfuss character in *Close Encounters* or the neighbourhood youngsters

LEFT John Cassavetes' Love Streams (1984) displayed some of his strengths and weaknesses as a director. his on-the-edge intensity and his rambling, rather self-indulgent style of narrative.

saving E.T. Spielberg's directorial touch used to be less certain in "adult" movies such as *The Color Purple* and *Always*, where the issues are more complex. However, the much admired and highly successful *Schindler's List* and *Saving Private Ryan*, with their massive and challenging subject matter, marked a new departure for him. In these films, both of which earned Spielberg Best Director Oscars, and despite their many faults, he could no longer be accused of an overly simplistic child's vision. *AI* (2001) was begun by Kubrick before he died

and completed by Spielberg. It is a film that lacks consistency. The opening sequences clearly show Kubrick's dark vision; the latter part is pure Spielberg – content sacrificed to visual effects and a whimsical sentimentality. However, Spielberg is a Hollywood phenomenon, not only

in terms of his success, but because he is a product of the very same movie culture which he now enriches. His faults as a director include a certain shallowness, the desire to please audiences at the expense of artistic integrity and the lack of real intellectual content.

ABOVE *Spielberg's* Saving Private Ryan *has an opening 20 minutes that communicates what war is really like more convincingly than almost any other war movie.*

BELOW *Spielberg's* Close Encounters of the Third Kind (1977) *represented aliens as benevolent beings.*

MARTIN SCORSESE (b. 1942)

Scorsese directed *Mean Streets* (1973) and *Taxi Driver* (1976), two of the seminal movies of the modern American cinema. Like the rest of the "movie brats", Scorsese is in love with cinema per se and his films persistently show his debt to old Hollywood. *Taxi Driver* is a very late *film noir, New York, New York* is in part a tribute to the MGM musical, *Raging Bull* owes something to *On the Waterfront* in its portrayal of the Jake La Motta protagonist, and *The Color of Money* is a late sequel to *The Hustler.* However, Scorsese brings his own personal obsessions to these movies: his ambivalence towards macho values, group and family loyalties, the concept of success and the price it demands. Several of his films have been criticized for their depiction of extreme violence, in particular *Mean Streets* (his first real success), *Taxi Driver, Raging Bull* and *GoodFellas. The Last Temptation of Christ* aroused great controversy amongst critics because of its perceived blasphemy.

Scorsese has consistently used his own experiences of growing up in the Little Italy section of New York as material in his films, and violence and Catholic guilt were intrinsic parts of that experience for him. He has a romantic trait and this comes out in *Alice Doesn't Live Here Any More* and *The Color of Money. King of Comedy* was

LEFT Taxi Driver is a seminal movie of the 1970s. Directed by Martin Scorsese and scripted by Paul Schrader, it is a vivid and compelling vision of urban life in that era.

a box-office failure but showed his talent for exposing through comedy the tawdry nature of the search for fame and success in modern America. In latter years, Scorsese seems to have run out of steam and *The Age of Innocence* (1993), *Casino* (1995) and *Bringing Out the Dead* (1999) smack of a director who has lost his way. *The Gangs of New York* (2002) returned to the themes of tribal loyalties and power-broking in the criminal world. Of all the so-called movie brats, Scorsese may turn out to be the most important as a maker of films that reflect their time. His films frequently make for uncomfortable viewing, partly because of the director's ambivalent attitude to his material, which, in turn, sets up insecurities in the spectator about how he or she should be reacting to the extreme emotions and violence represented on screen. The climax of *Taxi Driver* is a case in point: how do we react to the massacre of the bad guys by Travis Bickle (De Niro)? Raise a cheer or deplore such extreme vigilante actions? It is that kind of complexity that makes the best of Scorsese's movies memorable.

FRANCIS COPPOLA (b. 1939)

Coppola first made it in movies as a writer; his writing credits include *This Property is Condemned* and *Patton.* His first success as a director was *The Godfather,* which he also co-wrote, one of the key American movies of the 1970s. That was followed by the almost as impressive *The Conversation,* a movie about paranoia, betrayal and Nixon's America. *The Godfather Part II* (1974) was even more effective than the first part. Perhaps his most personal movie has been *Apocalypse Now,* an LSD picture of the Vietnam war. He sank a lot of the money he made out of the *Godfather* movies into this very expensive venture. He has, in fact, always been willing to risk his own capital, as shown when he founded his own studio, Zoetrope, in San Francisco and employed old Hollywood stalwart Gene Kelly and British director Michael Powell as associates, but this attempt to make films in a traditional studio-based set-up was doomed to failure. Movies such as *One from the Heart* and *Hammett* were more or less disasters at the box office, leaving Coppola relatively

BELOW The Godfather (1972) established Francis Coppola as a major director. Here the local undertaker seeks a favour from Don Corleone (Marlon Brando), the New York-based head of a Mafia family.

impoverished. He then made two teenage melodramas from S.E. Hinton novels, *The Outsiders* and *Rumble Fish*, which revived his fortunes, but failed to save the Zoetrope studios. *The Cotton Club* (1984) was a disaster, *Peggy Sue Got Married* (1986) a popular success but showed Coppola coasting, whilst *Tucker: The Man and His Dream* (1988) was disappointing. The third part of the *Godfather* trilogy followed in 1990: it has a stunning last 20 minutes, but it takes too long to reach that high dramatic point and cannot be compared in overall quality to the first two movies. *Bram Stoker's Dracula* (1992) lacked real conviction, whilst with *The Rainmaker* (1997) his career seemed finally to evaporate. Coppola's major achievements with the first two *Godfather* movies, *The Conversation* and *Apocalypse Now*, however, mean he has already won himself an important niche in Hollywood history. He has been a truly creative director, but like Orson Welles before him, has managed to dissipate his talent from a mixture of hubris, bad judgements and ill-luck.

BELOW *Oliver Stone wrote the screenplay of* Scarface *(1983), which was directed by Brian De Palma and starred Al Pacino. It is a very violent movie and was censured for that reason.*

OLIVER STONE (b. 1946)

As a writer, Stone was responsible for *Midnight Express*, *Scarface* and *Year of the Dragon*. He co-wrote and directed *Salvador*, a tough indictment of fascism in Latin America and America's covert support of it. Another film he wrote and directed, the Vietnam movie *Platoon*, won him an Oscar as a director; he had used his own experiences of the war as an ordinary "grunt" for his screenplay. *Wall Street* was another huge success for him as a director and writer; this time his target was greed and corruption among junk bond dealers, but the radicalism of the movie was watered down by pinning the blame on a few rotten apples rather than the system itself. This lack of political edge may be why Hollywood has taken Stone to its flinty bosom and showered further awards on his second Vietnam movie, *Born on the Fourth of July*, which showed a paraplegic Vietnam veteran winning through to become a public spokesman for his comrades.

However, *JFK* (1991), a long, rambling, and sometimes quite confusing but brilliant analysis of one of the many conspiracy theories surrounding John F. Kennedy's assassination, strengthened Stone's reputation for radicalism. Before that, he had made *The Doors*, a biopic about the rock star Jim Morrison. *Natural Born Killers* (1994) was wilfully misunderstood by many critics who criticized the movie for its violence, amorality and glamorization of young psychopathic killers. In fact, Stone intended it as an ironic statement about the media's obsession with crime and criminals and the way that the latter are turned into celebrities. The 1995 *Nixon* was a fascinating biopic of the former US president, which managed the dubious achievement of making you feel sorry for old Tricky Dicky. Stone's movies are usually a mixed bag: brilliance

ABOVE *Oliver Stone on the set of the 1993* Heaven and Earth. *Stone is one of the few important contemporary Hollywood directors prepared to break free from formulaic movie production, despite his sensationalist tendency.*

vying with indulgence and overstatement, intelligence competing with crassness and oversimplification. At the very least, they usually have a visceral quality that reflects the passions and energy of the director.

DAVID LYNCH (b. 1946)

The low-budget quasi-horror movie *Eraserhead* (1977) launched Lynch's career. He followed this with the more conventional *The Elephant Man* (1980) and then had a disastrous flop with the sci-fi bore *Dune* (1984). *Blue Velvet* (1986) and *Wild at Heart* (1990) re-established his credentials, while *Mulholland Drive* (2001) is considered by his fans to be a major opus of contemporary cinema. The *Twin Peaks* series on television won him a mass audience, but the movie sequel in 1992 was a mess. Indeed, there is a huge gap between the best and the worst of Lynch's work in the movies. For many, however, he is the most talented director working in contemporary Hollywood; for others, he is a pretentious and exploitative operator in the grey area between commercial schlock and art movies.

QUENTIN TARANTINO (b. 1963)

His many admirers compared the enfant terrible Tarantino with the young Orson Welles. His detractors, however, argue that his movies are all cool macho style and have little real significance. His detractors also assert that the films he has written and

ABOVE *Tarantino's* Reservoir Dogs *was shocking in its violence and sadism. Tarantino's ambivalence about torture and machismo makes for unsettling viewing.*

directed himself – *Reservoir Dogs* (1992), *Pulp Fiction* (1994) and *Jackie Brown* (1997) are basically splatter movies, selling designer violence to the mainly young and male masses. *Jackie Brown* – adapted from Elmore Leonard's novel *Rum Punch* – was a refreshing surprise, however. For a start, it has a much lower body count. Although it features Tarantino's trademark snappy dialogue, the characters have a depth and complexity missing from his earlier work. Pam Grier, whose star had waned since her 1970s "Blaxploitation" movies, clearly relishes a role that other actresses in their 40s would kill for. Only time will tell if Tarantino can abandon the cheap thrills of his early work and continue to produce

stories for thinking adults. He is undoubtedly talented, but appeals too often to the sadistic and the repressed violent, and possibly fascistic, impulses of the mass audience.

JAMES CAMERON (b. 1954)

Cameron made his directorial debut with the risible *Pirhana II: The Spawning* (1981). He first showed real promise with *The Terminator* (1984) – an unusually intelligent action movie. *Aliens* (1986), *The Abyss* (1989) and *Terminator 2: Judgment Day* (1991) all feature strong female characters, as well as what has become one of Cameron's hallmarks: ground-breaking use of state-of-the-art special effects. Cameron also works as a high-profile action screenwriter. His scripts include *Rambo: First Blood Part II* (1985) and *Strange Days* (1995). Cameron's detractors were certain that *Titanic* – at $200 million, the most expensive film ever made – would sink without trace. Instead, it became a box-office smash, winning 10 Oscars, including Best Director. *Titanic* is a

ABOVE *James Cameron directed the second of the* Alien *series with Sigourney Weaver as the intrepid Ripley.*

ABOVE *James Cameron had a huge success with* The Abyss, *an underwater sci-fi epic.*

visually stunning tribute to the doomed ship, but a movie should be more than just special effects. It is one of the worst Hollywood movies ever made, on a par with the horrendous *Pearl Harbor* (2000).

JOEL COEN (b. 1954) AND ETHAN COEN (b. 1957)

The Coen brothers started with the *film noir* thriller *Blood Simple* (1984) and have been making quirky, personal movies ever since. These include *Miller's Crossing* (1990), the very impressive *Barton Fink* (1991, one of the best movies about Hollywood ever made), *The Hudsucker Proxy* (1994), *Fargo* (1996), *The Big Lebowski* (1998) and *O Brother, Where Art Thou?* (2000), a modern version of Homer's *Odyssey*.

SPIKE LEE (b. 1957)

Lee is one of the few black directors to have reached major status within the Hollywood system. Movies such as *Do the Right Thing* (1989), *Mo' Better Blues* (1990), *Malcolm X* (1992) and *He Got Game* (1998) have garnered critical praise as well as large audiences.

RIGHT *Spike Lee not only directs, but also acts in a number of his own movies. Here he is with co-star Rosie Perez in* Do the Right Thing *(1989). Lee has sometimes been criticized for the sexual politics of his movies.*

RON HOWARD (b. 1954)

The 1984 *Splash!* was Howard's first real success and the banality of that movie set the tone for further success with *Cocoon* (1985), *Willow* (1988), *Backdraft* (1991), *Far and Away* (1992, starring Tom Cruise and Nicole Kidman), *Apollo 13* (1995) and *A Beautiful Mind* (2001).

TIM ROBBINS (b. 1958)

Robbins is better known as an actor, but he has directed three worthwhile movies: *Bob Roberts* (1992), in which he plays a phony country singer who uses his fame to run for office playing on the crude prejudices of his listening audience, *Dead Man Walking* (1995), a powerful indictment of capital punishment – a movie in which Sean Penn showed he really can act – and *The Cradle Will Rock* (1999), a movie version of the radical 1930s play first mounted by the left-wing Group Theatre.

MICHAEL MANN (b. 1943)

Michael Mann directed the first of the Hannibal Lecter movies, the 1986 *Manhunter* with Brian Cox as Lecter. He reaped the critical and commercial jackpot with the very effective adaptation of Fenimore Cooper's pre-Revolution in *The Last of the Mohicans* (1992). Basically, Mann is a storyteller of skill, as he showed once again in the overblown *Heat* (1995) and *The Insider* (1999).

ABOVE **The Last of the Mohicans** (*1992*) *gave Daniel Day-Lewis a marvellous part as Hawkeye, who performs heroics to rescue his love from the clutches of some very bad Native Americans indeed.*

"Houston, we have a problem."

RON HOWARD

APOLLO 13

LEFT *Perhaps Ron Howard's best movie was the impressive* Apollo 13 (*1995*), *about the real-life space mission that went badly wrong.*

INDEPENDENTS AND OUTSIDERS

MICHAEL CIMINO (b. 1943)

Is Michael Cimino merely a talented journeyman who happened to get lucky with subject, script and stars in *The Deer Hunter* (1978), one of the best films made in Hollywood in the 1970s? Before that, he had directed Clint Eastwood in the lightweight *Thunderbolt and Lightfoot* (1974) and after his huge success with the Vietnam movie, he became notorious for *Heaven's Gate* (1980), which reputedly ruined United Artists by costing millions over budget and taking minimal amounts at the box office. Since that debacle, Cimino has made the pedestrian *Year of the Dragon* (1985) and a remake of the old Bogart/Fredric March movie *The Desperate Hours* (1990).

JOHN SAYLES (b. 1950)

Sayles has been ploughing his particular furrow on the fringes of Hollywood for many years, making worthy, leftish movies about social issues. *Lianna* (1983) explored the theme of lesbianism long before mainstream Hollywood discovered designer lesbians. Sayles worked with radical cinematographer Haskell Wexler in the 1987 *Matewan* about coalminers' struggles in the 1920s and the following year he made *Eight Men Out*, a movie about the 1919 World Series baseball fix. The 1991 *City of Hope* deals with a more contemporary urban landscape narrative and as usual Sayles makes critical points about the injustices and hypocrisies of American life. *Lone Star* (1996) explored police corruption.

HAL HARTLEY (b. 1959)

Trust (1990) was perhaps Hartley's breakthrough movie, and since then he has established himself a comfortable niche in the independent, art-house circuit. *Simple Men* followed

ABOVE *Michael Cimino directed one of the best Vietnam movies* The Deer Hunter *(1978). Its central episode involves a very frightening game of Russian roulette.*

in 1992, then *Amateur* (1994), *Flirt* (1995) and *Henry Fool* (1997).

TODD SOLONDZ (b. 1959)

Solondz's reputation rests on two movies: *Welcome to the Dollhouse* (1995) and *Happiness* (1998). The former is a sharp and acerbic look at the constraints of family and suburban life on a teenage girl: it is definitely on the side of nonconformity and the nonjoiner. *Happiness* is rather an unpleasant and misanthropic movie that dwells with rather too much relish on perverse sexuality.

WHIT STILLMAN (b. 1952)

Stillman's characters are usually rich, Ivy League, sophisticated young men and women. Indeed, the characters in *Metropolitan* (1990) converse and interact with one another in such an intricate and urbane way that it comes over more as artifice than real. It is the same in the 1994 *Barcelona*: the characters he represents are so cool and cerebral that they seem to inhabit a different universe from mere mortals. The 1998 *The Last Days of Disco* is less etiolated, and some real pain filters through the sophistication, but his preppie world is beginning to pall somewhat and he will have to find a new impetus if he is to develop as a writer and director. His movies are intelligent, but somehow bloodless.

BRITISH DIRECTORS

CAROL REED (1906–76)

Carol Reed brought a liberal outlook to a conservative British film industry and made some of the most enduring of British films. His first major film was *The Stars Look Down* (1939) about coal miners. It starred Michael Redgrave as an idealistic coalminer's son who fights to win rights for the exploited miners. Reed also directed one of the great British movies, *Odd Man Out* (1947), which sympathetically portrayed an IRA gunman played by James Mason. *The Fallen Idol*, from a Graham Greene screenplay and

ABOVE *Carol Reed's* Odd Man Out (1947) *is a courageous British movie portraying an IRA activist in a sympathetic light.*

starring Ralph Richardson and Michèle Morgan, was expertly directed by Reed in 1948 and then he made his most famous film, *The Third Man*, with Orson Welles as the charming but criminal Harry Lime. *The Third Man* is generally thought to be one of the very best British movies ever made. *Outcast of the Islands*, adapted from the Conrad novel, was another distinguished film, although it is unfairly neglected nowadays. His later movies failed to match these successes, although *Oliver!* (1968) brought him a major international hit. Reed was one of the few British directors respected by the "movie brats" of Hollywood who admired his gifts.

MICHAEL POWELL (1905–90)

Working in collaboration with Emeric Pressburger, Powell directed some of the most colourful and interesting wartime and post-war British movies, including *The Thief of Bagdad* (1940), *The Life and Death of Colonel Blimp* (1943), *A Matter of Life and Death* (1946), *Black Narcissus* (1947) and *The Red Shoes* (1948). His films are distinguished by their elaborate design concepts, extravagant use of bright colour and a tendency towards lurid melodrama. He also made some awful movies such as *Oh, Rosalinda!* (1955), *Honeymoon* (1960) and *Age of Consent* (1969). A horror film made in 1960, *Peeping Tom*, was met by the almost total disapproval of critics and public, although Powell's reputation has been re-established and enhanced since then. Some of his earlier films are even more interesting than some of his much-praised later films: *The Edge of the World* (1937), *A Canterbury Tale* (1944) and *I Know Where I'm Going* (1945). Undoubtedly overrated as a

ABOVE *Rated by many as one of Michael Powell's best films,* The Red Shoes (1948) *incorporated a ballet sequence that exploited star Moira Shearer to the limit.*

director by people such as Martin Scorsese, Powell nevertheless was one of the most creative directors around in British cinema. At the very least, he tried to experiment in his films, and although his efforts are sometimes crass, he must be given credit for that.

ABOVE *Michael Powell co-directed* The Life and Death of Colonel Blimp (1943), *which reputedly was one of Churchill's favourite movies because it seemed to criticize the old guard of the military establishment.*

DAVID LEAN (1908–91)

Lean's first major success as a director was *Brief Encounter* (1946), that quintessential British tale of unconsummated illicit love set mainly in a railway station. There followed adaptations of two Dickens novels, which many think are Lean's best films: *Great Expectations* (1946) and *Oliver Twist* (1948). In the early 1950s he made *The Sound Barrier*, *Hobson's Choice* and *Summertime*, this last one starring Katharine Hepburn as a lovelorn spinster on holiday in Venice. He took a leap into the multi-million-dollar budget product with *The Bridge on the River Kwai* (1957), and from then it seemed that Lean could not make a small picture. *Lawrence of Arabia* (1962) and

Doctor Zhivago (1965) were two major successes for him, but his penchant for epic scale and overblown scenes served him badly in *Ryan's Daughter* (1970), a simple Irish love story that he attempted to inflate to epic dimensions. Critical raspberries for that film encouraged him to give up directing until he made *A Passage to India* in 1984, which was also received coolly, and was the last film he directed.

Lean was a director with a banal visual imagination (the success of movies such as *Lawrence of Arabia* owed a lot to his cinematographer, Freddie Young), but he had a certain talent for story-telling in the cinema, which probably came from his experience as a film editor. However, many people rate his films as serious movies worthy of earnest consideration. My advice is to wallow in movies such as *Zhivago* for what they are: overblown, enjoyable epics! *Lawrence of Arabia* alone will probably mean that his reputation will last.

LINDSAY ANDERSON (1923–94)

Anderson was first a critic, and then was involved in the "Free Cinema" British documentary movement, making many shorts in the 1950s, including *O Dreamland*, *Thursday's Children* and *Every Day Except Christmas*. His first feature was *This Sporting Life* (1963), a film about the northern working class and rugby league. This was followed by *If...* (1968), which was a huge success. Later movies were prone to high-minded sententiousness and to making "state-of-the-nation" simplifications. These include *O Lucky Man!* (1973) and *Britannia Hospital* (1982). Anderson's radicalism seemed to be transformed into a kind of nihilistic conservatism, throwing some doubt over how deeply felt his

OPPOSITE *David Lean directed* Doctor Zhivago *(1965), the highly successful epic film adaptation of Boris Pasternak's novel. Here Rod Steiger as the baddie seduces a fascinated Julie Christie.*

BELOW *This Sporting Life was directed by Lindsay Anderson and featured Richard Harris as an inarticulate rugby league player searching for emotional fulfilment in an affair with a widow played by Rachel Roberts.*

De quel côté serez-vous ? **if....**

RICHARD ATTENBOROUGH (b. 1923)

Attenborough had a long career as an actor in British films before turning to directing. He seems to be David Lean's natural successor in the overblown stakes. His first directorial effort, *Oh! What a Lovely War*, managed to depoliticize the message of the original stage version, which prepared the way for *Young Winston* (1972), a film supposedly about the youthful adventures of Churchill. *A Bridge Too Far* and *Magic* did not add much to his directorial reputation, but *Gandhi* (1982) did, and he won an Oscar for it. *A Chorus Line* (1985) was an unusual project for him, but he was back on more familiar territory with *Cry Freedom* (1987), which dealt with the story of black South African campaigner Steve Biko. *Chaplin* (1992) failed at the box office and largely with the critics.

Recently, he has been more active as a jobbing actor than as a director. He has reached that venerable age when he is treated with reverence by the Establishment. As a young actor, Attenborough would crop up in British war movies usually playing the working-class coward who broke down under pressure, much to the chagrin of the Public School officers. Dickie has come a long way from those roles. He may have been a better actor than a director, and will be remembered for his performances in *Brighton Rock* (1947) and *10 Rillington Place* (1971).

major works were. He returned to the theatre in the latter part of his life. The last movie he directed was *The Whales of August* (1987) with Bette Davis and Lillian Gish, a mediocre end to an interesting career in the cinema. He was a notoriously difficult man, dogmatic, egotistical and irritable, but he was an undoubted talent.

ABOVE *If... (1968) is generally considered to be Lindsay Anderson's major cinematic work. Its mix of revolutionary politics, teenage angst and a good deal of feyness makes it enduringly interesting. Anderson was a great movie buff, and If... was very heavily influenced by the work of Jean Vigo, the French director of Zéro de Conduite and L'Atalante.*

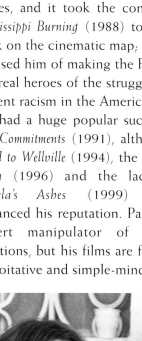

LEFT Oh! What a Lovely War, *directed by Richard Attenborough, was adapted from a stage play with music. It evoked the horror of the World War I trenches as though performed by a pierrot troupe on Brighton Pier.*

ALAN PARKER (b. 1944)

It was the success of the 1976 *Bugsy Malone* that established Parker as a director, and this led to his directing *Midnight Express* (1978), which was a huge hit and won him an Academy Award nomination. He even survived directing *Fame* (1980) and went on to make a very personal film about a marriage break-up, *Shoot the Moon* (1982), which starred Albert Finney and Diane Keaton. *Birdy* (1985) and *Angel Heart* (1987) did not make many waves, and it took the controversial *Mississippi Burning* (1988) to put him back on the cinematic map; his critics accused him of making the FBI agents the real heroes of the struggle against violent racism in the American South. He had a huge popular success with *The Commitments* (1991), although *The Road to Wellville* (1994), the execrable *Evita* (1996) and the lachrymose *Angela's Ashes* (1999) scarcely enhanced his reputation. Parker is an expert manipulator of audience emotions, but his films are frequently exploitative and simple-minded.

63

ABOVE Two new hopes of the 1970s *for British cinema: Alan Parker, director, and David Puttnam, producer.*

KEN LOACH (b. 1936)

Loach has been directing feature films for more than 30 years, so he can scarcely be called an emerging director, but it is only since around 1990 that he has been given sufficient credit for making movies with social and political messages from a leftist point of view. His TV play *Up the Junction* (1967), *Poor Cow* (1967), *Kes* (1969) and *Family Life* (1971) were all classic Loach works in which he represented working-class life with warmth and sympathy (usually) without falling into patronizing sentimentality. The 1980s were not fruitful for Loach and he seemed to become the forgotten man of British cinema in the Thatcher era, but *Hidden Agenda* (1990) and *Riff-Raff* (1990) brought him back into the fold. *Land and Freedom* (1995), *Carla's Song* (1996) and *My Name is Joe* (1998) all

BELOW *Ken Loach directed a young David Bradley in* Kes, *which was about a working-class boy's attempt to escape the brutality of his everyday life by caring for a kestrel.*

confronted political issues head-on. *Sweet Sixteen* (2002), however, seemed unnecessarily nihilist and hopeless in tone and subject. At times, Loach's movies seem more worthy in intent than remarkable in execution, but as almost a lone radical voice in the British cinema, he has to be lauded.

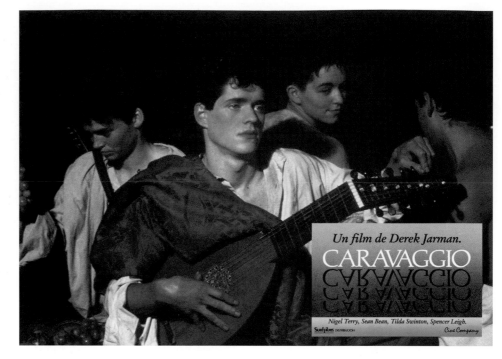

Un film de Derek Jarman.
CARAVAGGIO

Nigel Terry, Sean Bean, Tilda Swinton, Spencer Leigh.

ABOVE *Derek Jarman had a talent for the visual in the cinema, but did his movies amount to much more than that? This is a tableau from his movie* Caravaggio.

DEREK JARMAN (1942–94)

Jarman's first feature was *Sebastiane* (1976), followed by *Jubilee* (1978) and *The Tempest* (1979). *Caravaggio* (1986),

kes

Edward II (1991) and the 1993 Wittgenstein enhanced his reputation for directing movies that stressed the importance of decor and visual effects. Jarman died of Aids in 1994.

RIDLEY SCOTT (b. 1937)

Scott graduated from the world of television commercials to direct feature films. After The Duellists (1977), a film adaptation of a Joseph Conrad story, he had the good fortune to direct Alien (1979), the success of which placed him in the big league of bankable directors. This was followed by Blade Runner (1982), a movie that displayed Scott's talent for

RIGHT Ridley Scott's Blade Runner (1982) has become something of a cult movie for sci-fi fans. Certainly the sets and special effects are very impressive.

ABOVE The Draughtsman's Contract was a huge success for director Peter Greenaway. It is a movie that tries too hard to be "stylish".

creating impressive and rich visual effects. However, what his movies lack is food for the brain as Legend (1985), 1492: Conquest of Paradise (1992), Gladiator (2000) and Black Hawk Down (2001) prove. He also had a great success with Thelma and Louise (1991). There is no consistency in Scott's movies other than a kind of macho conservatism, but he is highly rated by some critics and movie fans.

PETER GREENAWAY (b. 1942)

Greenaway had his first big movie success with The Draughtsman's Contract (1983). This was followed by A Zed and Two Noughts (1985), Drowning by Numbers (1988) and The Cook, The Thief, His Wife and Her Lover (1989), all of them very arty or art-schooly. Prospero's Books, The Baby of Macon and The Pillow Book have continued to place emphasis on visuals rather than dramatic content.

MIKE LEIGH (b. 1943)

Leigh's movies often cover similar territory to Loach's but without the political conviction or warmth of the latter. His movies generally divide people into two camps: those who think he makes realistic and sometimes amusing films about the working- and lower-middle classes, and those who find his movies patronizing, smug, stereotyping and full of clichés. His first movie was Bleak Moments (1971), a very gloomy picture of social misfits in London guaranteed to make audiences feel smugly superior to these inadequate wretches. Nuts in May and Abigail's Party were popular successes on television, as Loach piled on the stereotypes and invited audiences to patronize these aspiring idiots. Secrets and Lies (1996) brought him to the attention of Hollywood, which Leigh

65

says he despises. The 2002 *All or Nothing* was an entirely nihilistic representation of working-class life on a London housing estate. Leigh is said to create his movies through extended improvisation with his actors and I have to say that this shows. Many of the performances in the movies he has directed can only be described as examples of "coarse acting" at its coarsest. Cinemagoers beg to differ, so Leigh will continue to prosper.

SAM MENDES (b. 1965)

Mendes directed *American Beauty* in 1999, a movie that won several Oscars and was a box-office success. For me, it was a shallow movie, glib, superficial and pretentious. *Road to Perdition* (2002) had the misfortune to have Tom Hanks cast as a hitman, but

BELOW *Mike Leigh directed this grim tale,* Naked. *Katrin Cartlidge and Lesley Sharp share their troubles over a glass of beer.*

that is not the only reason the film sinks almost without trace. Mendes goes for "style", drowning routine Mafia material in a sea of self-conscious and arty visual effects. However, Mendes is undoubtedly going to be a major player in the movie world if that is what he wants to do with his directing career.

LYNNE RAMSAY (b. 1969)

With *Ratcatcher* and *Morvern Callar*, Lynne Ramsay has raised expectations that a major new directing talent is emerging. In the male-dominated world of movie-making and directing, it is encouraging to see female directors such as Ramsay making a breakthrough into mainstream film-making. She seems a distinctive voice and is prepared to take some risks.

OTHER NOTABLES

Other significant British directors include: Thorold Dickinson (1903–84), who directed *Queen of*

Spades (1949) and *Secret People* (1952); Anthony Asquith (1902–68), who made *The Way to the Stars* (1945), *The Winslow Boy* (1948), *The Browning Version* (1950), *The Importance of Being Earnest* (1951) and *Orders to Kill* (1958); Tony Richardson (1928–91), director of the "new" British school of the 60s, who made *The Entertainer* (1960), *A Taste of Honey* (1961), *The Loneliness of the Long-Distance Runner* (1963), *Tom Jones* (1963), *The Loved One* (1965), *The Charge of the Light Brigade* (1968) and *The Border* (1982); John Schlesinger (b. 1926), who came to prominence with his documentary about Waterloo Station, *Terminus* (1961), and then went on to direct *A Kind of Loving* (1962), *Billy Liar* (1963), *Darling* (1965), *Far from the Madding Crowd* (1967), *Midnight Cowboy* (1969), *Sunday Bloody Sunday* (1971), *The Day of the Locust* (1975), *Marathon Man* (1976), *Yanks* (1979), *Honky Tonk Freeway* (1981) and *An Englishman Abroad* (1983).

FRENCH DIRECTORS

MARCEL CARNÉ (1909–96)

Carné was the most important French director of the immediate pre-World War II and Occupation years, directing a number of poetic and atmospheric melodramas that somehow made statements about France and its situation. *Drôle de Drame* (1937), *Le Quai des Brumes* (1938) and *Le Jour Se Lève* (1939) are three classics of the French cinema. Who can forget Jean Gabin as the decent working-class man holding out against the massed forces of law and order in *Le Jour Se Lève?* Gabin also starred in *Le Quai des Brumes* with Michel Simon and a very young Michèle Morgan. It is a melancholy film, somehow capturing the unease and sadness of an immediate pre-war France. *Les Enfants du Paradis* is a parable about the Occupation made right under German noses in 1944; it has Jean-Louis Barrault as a milksop mime artist, Pierre Brasseur as an exhibitionistic actor and sundry 19th-century nasties (who stood in for the Nazis), all quarrelling over Arletty, who represented France. Carné's post-war movies were not of the same standard, almost certainly because, apart from *Les Portes de la Nuit* (1946), he was no longer collaborating with screenwriter Jacques Prévert, who had written the screenplays for his most memorable movies.

JEAN RENOIR (1894–1979)

Jean was the son of the painter, Auguste Renoir; he had a long and distinguished career in the French cinema right from the silent years through to the late 1960s. His best-known films include *La Chienne*,

Boudu Sauvé des Eaux, Le Crime de Monsieur Lange, Les Bas-fonds, Une Partie de Compagne and two classics, *La Grande Illusion* and *La Règle du Jeu*. During the war and the post-war years, he made films in Hollywood which included *The Southerner*, *The Diary of a Chambermaid* and *The Woman on the Beach*. Later movies were *The River*, *The Golden Coach* and *Picnic on the Grass*. Like Carné, Renoir peaked around the

ABOVE *Marcel Carné's major directing achievement is* Les Enfants du Paradis, *made during the German occupation of Paris.*

late 1930s and he will be remembered for *La Grande Illusion* and *La Règle du Jeu*. There is a likeable humanism to the movies he made and they were mostly intelligently directed and written. Perhaps his movies are too literary for the purist.

JEAN-LUC GODARD (b. 1930)

When Godard made *À Bout de Souffle* (*Breathless*) in 1960, he became the doyen of the "New Wave" of French directors. His innovative techniques – jump cuts, hand-held cameras, a semi-documentary approach and a disregard for "normal" narrative – helped him to "genius director" status. Subsequent films also gained a great deal of attention: *Une Femme est une Femme, Vivre Sa Vie, Le Petit Soldat, Les Carabiniers, Bande à Part, Une Femme Mariée, Alphaville* and *Le Mépris.* Like most of the New Wave directors, Godard was besotted with the American cinema, especially *film noir* and "B" movies. However, around the mid-1960s he went down with a bad case of Mao-itis and his films have

> "FILM IS TRUTH 24 TIMES A SECOND."
> *JEAN-LUC GODARD*

never really recovered. In his attempts to interrupt classical story-telling in the cinema and hammer home political points, he has become a bore. He is quoted as saying, "My aesthetic is that of the sniper on the roof"; the trouble is that he is shooting himself in the foot.

BELOW *Les Carabiniers is a typical Godard movie of the 1960s. Dispensing with conventional narrative, it makes polemical points by inviting the audience to distance itself emotionally from the characters' actions.*

FRANÇOIS TRUFFAUT (1932–84)

If Godard was the Marxist conscience of the French New Wave, Truffaut was its soft centre. A rather self-conscious charm oozed from his films and this sometimes edges over into preciousness and sentimentality. However, his best films had an edge to them that belied his innately gentle nature: *Les Quatre Cent Coups, Shoot the Pianist, Jules et Jim, Fahrenheit 451, L'Enfant Sauvage, Anne and Muriel, La Nuit Américaine, Le Dernier Métro* and *Vivement Dimanche.* Truffaut also made a memorable appearance in Spielberg's

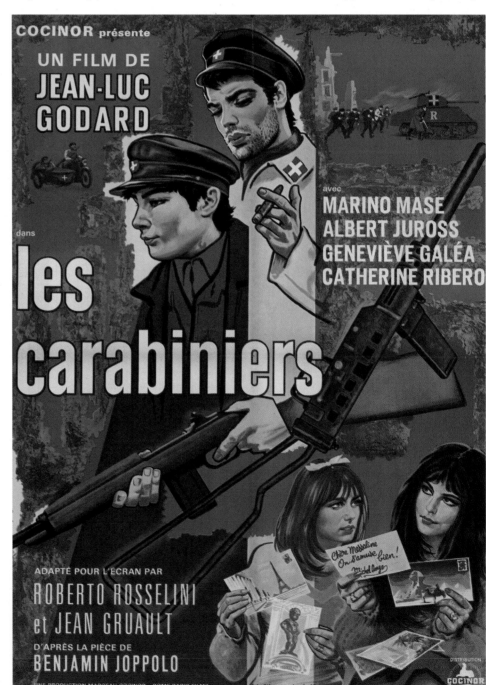

ABOVE *Jean-Luc Godard explored femininity and the reality of women's lives in a number of movies, including* Vivre Sa Vie *(1962), which starred Anna Karina.*

JULIE **CHRISTIE** · OSKAR **WERNER**

FAHRENHEIT 451

TECHNICOLOR®

ALSO STARRING **CYRIL CUSACK**
ANTON **DIFFRING** JEREMY **SPENSER** ALEX **SCOTT**
SCREENPLAY BY FRANCOIS TRUFFAUT & JEAN-LOUIS RICHARD · BASED ON THE NOVEL BY RAY BRADBURY · EXECUTIVE PRODUCER LEWIS M. ALLEN

DIRECTED BY **FRANCOIS TRUFFAUT**

A VINEYARD FILMS LIMITED PRODUCTION · A UNIVERSAL-INTERNATIONAL RELEASE

Close Encounters of the Third Kind as the only scientist who was sympathetic to the ordinary people who tried to make direct contact with the aliens.

LOUIS MALLE (1932–95)
One of the French New Wave in the 1950s, Malle survived as a major director into the 90s. His first film, *L'Ascenseur pour l'Echafaud*, was a Hitch-cockian thriller with an improvised jazz score by Miles Davis. *Les Amants* caused a furore in the late 50s because it showed a wealthy bourgeois French wife and mother (Jeanne Moreau) abandoning husband and children for a lover who has introduced her to sensual pleasures. Most of his other films also explored controversial territory. *Le Feu Follet* was a brooding, pessimistic study of the last day in the life of a self-destructive writer, while *Viva Maria* was, by contrast, a rather mindless romp starring Moreau and

ABOVE *Francois Truffaut directed Oskar Werner and Julie Christie in* Fahrenheit 451 *(1966), a bleak glimpse of a bookless future. It would have been more interesting if Jean-Luc Godard had directed it.*

Brigitte Bardot. *Le Souffle au Coeur* explored the theme of incestuous feelings between mother and son, while *Pretty Baby*, his first American film, dealt with child prostitution. Both of his best films – *Lacombe Lucien* and *Au Revoir les Enfants* – dealt with aspects of the French Occupation. *Atlantic City*, with Burt Lancaster, was another American film – an interesting treatment on the theme of regeneration. *My Dinner with André* was about two men talking in a restaurant about life and regeneration (again). *Damage* (1992) and *Uncle Vanya on 42nd Street* (1994) were his last movies. Malle was a curious mixture of deeply-felt emotion and a shallow chicness.

ABOVE *One of Claude Chabrol's most effective psychological thrillers is* Le Boucher *(1969), about a serial killer in a small French town.*

CLAUDE CHABROL (b. 1930)

Most of the New Wave directors revered Hitchcock as "the master" and none more so than Chabrol, many of whose films are very Hitchcockian and full of Catholic obsessions about transference of guilt and punishment. After his early successes with *Le Beau Serge* and *Les Cousins*, Chabrol directed *Les Biches*, *La Femme Infidèle*, *Le Boucher*,

Violette Nozière, *L'Enfer*, *Blood Relatives*, *Cop au Vin* and *Inspector Lavardin*. The quality of his films varies enormously (he managed to make *Madame Bovary* (1991) extremely tedious), but his forte is murder within a French bourgeois setting, with or without adulterous connotations.

JACQUES TATI (1908–82)

Tati carried the tradition of silent-screen comedy into sound movies. His best films, *Jour de Fête* (1949), *Monsieur Hulot's Holiday* (1952), *Mon Oncle* (1958) and *Traffic* (1961), are practically wordless. He avoids the pathos of Chaplin and Keaton and his movies are the better for that. Tati's movies divide audiences: there are those who think he is a comic genius both as director and actor; others can watch his movies without laughing.

LEFT *Jacques Tati starred in and directed some of the most popular French comedies ever made: they included* Jour de Fête, Monsieur Hulot's Holiday, Mon Oncle *and* Traffic.

RIGHT *Patrice Leconte, the French director of* The Hairdresser's Husband *and* L'Homme du Train, *on location.*

BERTRAND TAVERNIER (b. 1941)

A classic French film director, Tavernier's films have frequently had Philippe Noiret as their star: *The Watchmaker of St Paul's*, *Coup de Torchon*, *A Sunday in the Country*, *Round Midnight*, *Life and Nothing But*, *These Foolish Things* and *Laissez-Passer*. Tavernier is in the radical tradition of French cinema and he seldom makes a movie that is less than interesting.

PATRICE LECONTE (b. 1947)

Monsieur Hire (1989) and *The Hairdresser's Husband* (1990) established Leconte as the director of quirky, "small" movies that take a healthy

interest in sexual foibles. *Ridicule* (1996) presented a larger canvas to Leconte and he scored with his representation of intrigues at the French court. The 2002 *L'Homme Du Train* concentrated once more on relationships, this time between a loner criminal and a seemingly respectable retired schoolteacher. Leconte makes intimate movies about outsiders and obsessives.

CLAUDE BERRI (b. 1934)

Berri had directed numerous feature films before he had a huge success with *Jean de Florette* (1986) and the sequel *Manon des Sources* from the same

year. He followed that with *Uranus* (1990), a laudable attempt to deal with the running sore of the German Occupation years in France. *Germinal* (1993) was adapted from the Zola novel and starred Gérard Depardieu.

MATHIEU KASSOVITZ (b. 1967)

Kassovitz is an actor turned director, and he made one of the best French movies of the 1990s, *La Haine*, which focused on three young men from a Parisian housing estate determined to get their revenge on a violent, sadistic and racist police force.

ABOVE Jour de Fête (1949) was Jacques Tati's first major international success. He played a village postman who has dreams of speeding up his delivery with American-type methods.

ITALIAN DIRECTORS

VITTORIO DE SICA (1902–74)

De Sica was best known to the general public as a comedy actor, but he was also one of the leading directors of the post-war Italian Neo-realist school who influenced directors in the rest of Europe and in Hollywood. His most famous film is *Bicycle Thieves* (1948); set amidst the poverty of post-war Italy, it concerns the theft of a bicycle from a working-class man who needs it desperately to carry out his treasured job as a bill-poster. The film may be sentimental in parts, but it would take a heart of stone not to be touched by the scene where the bill-poster's young son defends his beleaguered father when an angry crowd turns on him after he is forced to steal another man's bicycle to make up for the loss of his own. *Shoeshine* (1946) and *Umberto D* (1952) were two other Neo-realist classics, but of the later films he directed, only *Two Women* (1960) with Sophia Loren and the 1972 *The Garden of the Finzi-Continis*

BELOW By the time Vittoria De Sica made Gold of Naples (1954), he had abandoned Neo-realism and used glamorous stars such as Silvana Mangano and Sophia Loren.

made much of an impact. Neo-realism aimed to present a naturalistic picture of the lives of ordinary people using actual locations and avoiding the sentimentality and narrative structures of the commercial cinema. Frequently, amateur actors were used rather than professionals.

ROBERTO ROSSELLINI (1906–77)

Rossellini was the other leading director of the Neo-realists, but he became famous for other reasons – his affair with, and subsequent marriage to, Ingrid Bergman. A documentary style, the use of a mixture of amateur and professional actors, a refusal to glamorize, a radical social viewpoint – these are the characteristics of Rossellini's films such as *Open City, Paisà, Stromboli, Europa '51* and *Louis XIV Seizes Power*. The fashion for Neo-realism passed relatively quickly, and Rossellini never found a niche in the commercial cinema.

ABOVE Here Federico Fellini megaphones his instructions to the cast and crew on one of the elaborate sets of his 1987 film, Intervista.

LUCHINO VISCONTI (1906–76)

Visconti's early films, such as *Ossessione* (1942) and *La Terra Trema* (1948), were heavily influenced by Neo-realism, but he soon abandoned that for an operatic, bravura style in movies such as *Senso* (1954), *Rocco and his Brothers* (1960), *The Leopard* (1963), *The Damned* (1969) and *Death in Venice* (1971). A former art director, Visconti seemed at times to indulge his taste for opulent sets and costumes at the expense of his films' thematic content. He also directed operas, and this shows in the over-emotionalism that mars some of his movies.

FEDERICO FELLINI (1920–93)

Fellini's early films were clearly influenced by Neo-realism: *I Vitelloni* (1953), *La Strada* (1954) and *Il Bidone* (1955). In these movies Fellini was

OPPOSITE Fellini's 1960 movie La Dolce Vita satirized Roman high society. It starred Mastroianni as a jaundiced journalist and Anita Ekberg as a film star whose character was based closely on herself.

UN FILM PONTI - DE LAURENTIIS PRODOTTO DA DINO DE LAURENTIIS E CARLO PONTI PRODUTTORE ESECUTIVO MARCELLO GIROSI

SILVANA **MANGANO** *in* **L'ORO DI NAPOLI** *un film di* **VITTORIO DE SICA** *con*

SOPHIA LOREN EDUARDO DE FILIPPO PAOLO STOPPA ERNO CRISA

SOGGETTO TRATTO DAL LIBRO OMONIMO DI **GIUSEPPE MAROTTA** E CON LA ECCEZIONALE PARTECIPAZIONE DI **TOTO'** REGIA CINEMATOGRAFICA DI **CESARE ZAVATTINI**

Angelo Rizzoli
présente
stelt voor

JULIETTA MASINA
SANDRA MILO
VALENTINA CORTESE
SYLVA KOSCINA

un film de
een film van
FELLINI

JULIETTE
des   der
ESPRITS✦GEESTEN

Distr. FRANCORIZ

Affiches "WIK" TEL. 43.88.92 - Bruxelles 18

LEFT *Fellini directed his wife Giulietta Masina in the 1965* Juliet of the Spirits, *a movie you either love or loathe.*

clearly drawing on autobiographical material and using backgrounds and a way of life he knew intimately. However, once he became an international name and the fashion for Neo-realism passed, he discarded Neo-realism to make highly personal and exhibitionistic movies, including

films such as *La Dolce Vita, Boccaccio 70, 8½* (which was an extended reflection on himself as a director), *Juliet of the Spirits* (which people either hate or love), *Satyricon, Fellini's Roma, Amarcord* and *Ginger and Fred. 8½* is a brilliant movie in many ways, but it also marked a dead-end for the

director. Thereafter, he was parodying himself and being self-consciously "Fellini-esque". Fellini's world is a world of dreams and fantasies; he is consumed with memories of his childhood and his relationship with Catholicism. At his best he was skilful at depicting the uncertainties of

ABOVE *Michelangelo Antonioni lines up a shot from behind the camera. The composition of the image within the frame was extremely important to this director.*

human relationships, at his worst he was showily indulgent and modish. Feminists, on the whole, dislike his movies because he treats women as objects while pretending to worship them. After 8½, he scarcely made a decent film; perhaps he was right in depicting the director in the movie (clearly intended to be a self-portrait) as having run out of ideas.

MICHELANGELO ANTONIONI (b. 1912)

Antonioni came to international prominence with *L'Avventura* (1960), then went on to make *La Notte* and *L'Eclisse*. The 1966 *Blowup* was a

RIGHT *Antonioni directed David Hemmings and Vanessa Redgrave in the 1966* Blowup, *a bleak picture of "swinging London".*

commercial success for him, and this led MGM to give him the money to make *Zabriskie Point*, which failed at the box office. He made *The Passenger* with Jack Nicholson in 1975, his last important movie. Later movies, *The Oberwald Mystery*, *Identification of a Woman* and *Beyond the Clouds*, are fairly unengaging attempts to expand the boundaries of film beyond narrative

coherence and continuity. Antonioni is an intellectual whose films explore bourgeois aridity and questions of identity. The pace of his films is slow and the dialogue is sparse. He creates images that encapsulate the thematic content of the film. For directing *L'Avventura* alone, he will always have an honoured place in film history.

BERNARDO BERTOLUCCI (b. 1940)

Bertolucci has left-wing views that inform most of his early films. One of his best is *The Conformist* with Jean-Louis Trintignant as a fascist, and a study of fascism also makes both parts of *1900* interesting social documents. He made the contro-versial *Last Tango in Paris* with Marlon Brando and Maria Schneider in 1972, and *La Luna* with Jill Clayburgh in 1979. He had a surprising success with *The Last Emperor* which is not, however, one of his better films. *The Sheltering Sky* was a worthy attempt to translate Paul Bowles's novel to the screen, but his later films such as *Little Buddha* and especially *Stealing Beauty* mark a steady deterioration in his powers as a director. He seems to have been seduced by the more superficial aspects of the movie world in his later works.

GIUSEPPE TORNATORE (b. 1956)

Tornatore had a major worldwide success with the 1988 *Cinema Paradiso*, a success which he has been unable to replicate in subsequent movies. Later movies include *Especially on Sundays*, *A Pure Formality*, *The Star Maker* and *The Legend of the Pianist on the Ocean*.

ROBERTO BENIGNI (b. 1952)

Benigni was better known as an actor before he wrote and directed *Johnny Stecchino* (1991), which proved an enormous box-office success in Italy but is virtually unknown outside of it. However, with *Life is Beautiful* (1998) he achieved worldwide fame and success. This is a movie that definitely divides audiences: there are those who see it a warmly humanistic tribute to the human spirit in the face of the nightmare of Nazi concentration camps and those who see it as a trivializing, exploitative and crassly

ABOVE *The frank sexuality of Bertolucci's* Last Tango in Paris *caused much controversy when the film was released in* 1972. *It starred Marlon Brando and Maria Schneider.*

sentimental picture of the Holocaust. Benigni's best-known movies as an actor (apart from *Life is Beautiful*) are *Down by Law* (1986) and *Night on Earth* (1991), both directed by Jim Jarmusch, and the abysmal *Son of the Pink Panther* (1993).

ABOVE *Bertolucci directed John Malkovich and Debra Winger in his adaptation of the Paul Bowles novel* The Sheltering Sky.

ABOVE *Pier Paolo Pasolini (1922–75) was a controversial Italian film director. He directed* The Arabian Nights *in* 1974.

GERMAN DIRECTORS

FRITZ LANG (1890–1976)

Lang will always be remembered for having directed *Metropolis* (1927), a dark picture of a technologically advanced but oppressive society. His two *Dr Mabuse* movies also enhanced his reputation, but his leftist leanings did not endear him to Hitler's henchmen, and he left Germany in the early 1930s to work in Hollywood, where he made the noteworthy *Fury* in 1936. In the 1940s he directed *The Woman in the Window* and *Ministry of Fear*, while in the 1950s he made *Rancho Notorious*, *The Big Heat* and *Beyond a Reasonable Doubt*. He played himself in Jean-Luc Godard's 1963 *Le Mépris* (*Contempt*), a cynical view of Hollywood values.

LENI RIEFENSTAHL (b. 1902)

Riefenstahl will always be remembered for two movies: *Triumph of the Will* (1934), which filmed one of the Nazis' Nuremberg Rallies, and *The Olympiad* (1938). Undoubtedly an extremely talented director, Riefenstahl allowed herself to be used

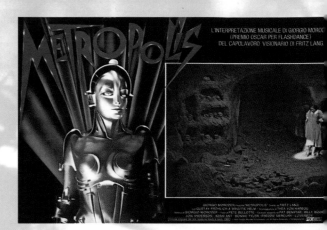

RIGHT *Fritz Lang's most famous movie is* Metropolis, *an outstanding example of German expressionism of the 1920s, evoking a bleak picture of the future, which in some ways forecast Nazi horrors.*

by the Nazi propaganda machine, for which she has never been forgiven by her own people. Her two movie "masterpieces" raise important questions about how we evaluate film: is the power of, say, *Triumph of the Will* to be denied because it was an instrument of a vile regime? Can we stand back from the content and intention behind a piece of film and admire the artistry that created it?

RAINER WERNER FASSBINDER (1946–82)

Fassbinder was a fashionable director of the 1970s, but it remains to be seen whether the films he made stand the test of time. Personally, I could not bear to sit through *The Bitter Tears of Petra Von Kant* again, but Fassbinder undoubtedly has his supporters. His best-known films are *Effi Briest*, *Fear Eats the Soul*, *Despair*, *The Marriage of Maria Braun* and his TV mini-series *Berlin Alexanderplatz*. The last two are the most accessible of his works.

WERNER HERZOG (b. 1942)

Herzog is an obsessive film-maker and he often makes films that are about obsessives, such as the Klaus Kinski protagonist in *Fitzcarraldo*, who is determined to bring grand opera to the jungles of South America. His first major success was *Aguirre: The Wrath of God* (1973), but before that he had made *Even Dwarfs Started Small* and *Fata Morgana*. *The Enigma of Kasper Hauser* attracted a good deal of attention, as did his version of the legend of Dracula, *Nosferatu the Vampyre*, which reflected Murnau's silent original. Apart from *Fitzcarraldo*, the 1980s did

not bring him much success. He is quoted as saying that he is not out to win prizes, which he considers to be suitable only for dogs and horses.

WIM WENDERS (b. 1945)

Wenders makes odd, often slow-paced movies that frequently pay some kind of oblique homage to Hollywood, but are described as pretentious by his detractors. *Kings of the Road* and *The American Friend*, for example, are recognizably reworkings of the road movie and thriller genres. In the latter, he gives a part to the cult American director, Nicholas Ray; then, in *Lightning over Water*, the subject is Ray himself during the last few months of his life. Francis Coppola employed Wenders to direct *Hammett* at Coppola's Zoetrope Studio – a convoluted treatment of *film noir* themes that involved a representation of Dashiel Hammett himself. But there were great difficulties during the making of the film, and it is not clear how much of the final movie was directed by Wenders. *The Goalkeeper's Fear of the Penalty*, one of Wenders' first films, at least has a novel title. *Alice in the Cities* attracted attention, while *Paris, Texas* achieved minor box-office success and made a star of Harry Dean Stanton. He co-directed the 1995 *Beyond the Clouds* with Michaelangelo Antonioni and in 1999 he had a success with *Buena Vista Social Club*.

AUSTRALIAN DIRECTORS

PETER WEIR (b. 1944)

Weir's first big success was *Picnic at Hanging Rock* (1975), one of the first films of the 1970s to signal the revival in Australian cinema. It is an

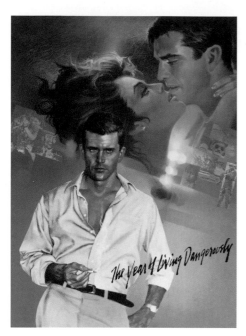

ABOVE The Year of Living Dangerously (*1982*), *which starred Mel Gibson and Sigourney Weaver, was an international success for Australian director Peter Weir.*

evocative, "arty" and resonant film that raises more issues than it can adequately deal with, but it is still a real achievement. Weir followed this up with *The Last Wave* (1977), which again had mystical and religious elements and tried to explore Australian guilt about the Aborigines. *Gallipoli* (1981) to a certain extent dealt with the theme of what it is to be an Australian. Weir's first big-budget movie was one of the key films of the 1980s: *The Year of Living Dangerously* (1982) with Mel Gibson and Sigourney Weaver, and Linda Hunt memorably cast as a male dwarf. It is about the conflict between the drive to succeed and the need to commit yourself to loving another person. After that success he directed Harrison Ford in *Witness* (1985) and

The Mosquito Coast (1986). Both of these films, and others he has directed, deal in part with culture clash, and have a charismatic figure representing some kind of life force at the centre of the narrative. This is certainly true of the Robin Williams character in *Dead Poets Society* (1989), which was another big success. However, his 1990 film *Green Card*, with that other life force Gérard Depardieu, may be thought of as somewhat disappointing from a director who has made such unusual movies to date. However, with the 1993 *Fearless* and the 1998 *The Truman Show*, Weir returned to form.

JANE CAMPION (b. 1955)

Campion is a New Zealander by birth, but has worked mostly in the Australian film industry. Her sensitive direction of *An Angel at my Table* (1990) marked her down as a director worth watching and she followed that up with *The Piano* (1993), which starred Holly Hunter (she won the

ABOVE *Holly Hunter plays a mute Scottish emigrant to New Zealand in Jane Campion's* The Piano. *Campion also wrote the script.*

Best Actress Oscar) and became an international hit. *The Portrait of a Lady* (1996) starred Nicole Kidman and was an adaptation of the Henry James novel; it was unfairly savaged by the critics and it seems Campion's career has still to recover from that failure.

BAZ LUHRMANN (b. 1962)

Luhrmann's first big success was with *Strictly Ballroom* (1992) and he followed that up with his movie of *Romeo and Juliet* (1996), which starred Leonardo DiCaprio and made Shakespeare accessible to teenage

ABOVE *Baz Luhrmann's first big success was with* Strictly Ballroom, *a satire on ballroom dancing competitions and their participants.*

audiences. However, it was with *Moulin Rouge* (2001) that Luhrmann really hit the big time. This reworking of the movie musical divided audiences and critics: you either love or hate it. Undoubtedly Luhrmann is a talented director, but whether he can graduate from cinematic pyrotechnics and high camp frolics to more challenging material remains to be seen. Perhaps style is all to Luhrmann.

FIVE INTERNATIONAL DIRECTORS

INGMAR BERGMAN (b. 1918)

Bergman is a Swedish writer-director who first came to international prominence with his medieval allegory, *The Seventh Seal* (1957). This success led to the release outside Sweden of earlier films such as *Summer with Monika*, *Sawdust and Tinsel* and *Smiles of a Summer Night*. *Wild Strawberries* was another major film in 1957. Bergman's films tend to the austere and gloomy, notably in *The Virgin Spring*, *Through a Glass Darkly* and *The Silence*. Bergman is wrestling with his doubts about the existence of God; if God does exist, he seems to say, why are evil deeds and such cruelty allowed to happen?

Women are very often the central protagonists in his movies, for example in *Persona*, *Cries and Whispers* and *Autumn Sonata*. The impossibility

Bergman's characteristic blend of austere Calvinism and fear of punishment for sins that have been committed.

Working with a distinguished repertory company of actors drawn from Stockholm's Royal Academy Theatre, Bergman drew fine performances from actors such as Max Von Sydow, Gunnar Björnstrand, Liv Ullmann, Harriet Anderson, Ingrid Thulin and Erland Josephson. Bergman is the "art house" director par excellence, but his movies are both

"entertaining" and involving with an emotional intensity that is disturbing at times. Bergman must rank as one of the most talented directors ever to have worked in the medium. He is also an extremely creative stage director.

Bergman usually writes his own screenplays, imposing his personal vision on the subject matter. As he has created considerable independence for himself, he of all directors can surely be seen as an auteur.

AKIRA KUROSAWA (1910–98)

The Japanese director built up an international following with *Rashomon* (1950) and *Seven Samurai* (1954), the latter remade in Hollywood as

ABOVE *Ingmar Bergman made several movies with Liv Ullmann, including the dark, violent film* The Shame (1968).

of man–woman relationships and bourgeois marriage is a recurring theme. However, *Fanny and Alexander* revealed a warmer, more humanistic side to his artistic personality when he used affectionate memories of his Stockholm childhood to paint an evocative picture of extended family life. Mixed in with this, however, is

ABOVE *The 1972* Cries and Whispers, *directed by Ingmar Bergman, starred Erland Josephson and Liv Ullmann.*

79

ABOVE *Akira Kurosawa's* Rashomon *(1950) won the Golden Lion at the 1951 Venice Film Festival. The picture was remade by director Martin Ritt in 1964 as* The Outrage.

The Magnificent Seven. Later films such as *Throne of Blood* and *The Hidden Fortress* reinforced his reputation for action movies within the samurai tradition; he was often likened to John Ford. His later films were highly praised but seem too leisurely and indulgent for some tastes, as if he had become too conscious of his artistic status, as in, for example, *The Shadow Warrior* and *Ran.* Apart from his samurai epics, he directed modern-day pictures, including the impressive *Living* and *The Lower Depths.*

ANDREI TARKOVSKY (1932–86)

Some people would rather watch paint dry than sit through one of this late Russian director's films again; others see Tarkovsky as a genius of the modern cinema. He died in 1986 at the age of 54, having directed a handful of long, slow-paced arty

RIGHT *Andrei Tarkovsky's movie* Andrei Rublev *(1966) is about a medieval painter, but can be interpreted as being about the role of the artist in a repressive regime such as the Soviet Union under communism.*

movies that elevated him to major auteur status in many people's minds. In constant bother with the pre-glasnost Soviet authorities, Tarkovsky first came to prominence with *Andrei Rublev* (1966), then directed an obscure movie about space, *Solaris* (1972), that won the jury prize at the Cannes Film Festival. *Mirror* and *Nostalgia* were more overtly

ABOVE *The 1965* Repulsion *explored classic Polanski territory: repressed sexuality and the havoc such repression causes.*

personal and political statements. It is tragic that Tarkovsky died before the present thaw in the Soviet Union happened; it would have been interesting to see what kind of movies he would have made in his homeland in the new circumstances.

ROMAN POLANSKI (b. 1933)

Polanski first came to international prominence when he directed *Knife in the Water* (1962). Thereafter, he made all of his films outside his native Poland. His films are full of violence, sexual quirks and the occult. *Repulsion* and *Cul-de-Sac* are odd, claustrophobic studies of repression. He had a major Hollywood success with *Rosemary's Baby*, which dealt with devil-worship. Tragically, Polanski's own life became inextricably linked with the macabre and the occult when his wife Sharon Tate was one of the victims of ritual murder at the hands of the Charles Manson "family".

Polanski's version of *Macbeth* emphasized witchery and violence, while *Chinatown* was a brilliant reworking of *film noir* themes. Polanski has also had his out-and-out

commercial flops, including *What?* and *Pirates*. *Tess* was a surprisingly subdued version of the Thomas Hardy novel, *The Tenant* explored themes of gender and identity, and *Frantic* was only a partially successful thriller starring Harrison Ford. Along the way Polanski picked up a charge of statutory rape in America for allegedly sleeping with a minor, which means he must work abroad unless he is prepared to stand trial in America. In the 1990s he directed *Bitter Moon*, *Death and the Maiden* and *The Ninth Gate*, then won a Best Director Oscar for *The Pianist* (2002).

SATYAJIT RAY (1921–92)

Ray's *Apu* trilogy in the 1950s put Indian cinema firmly on the international film map. *Pather Panchali*, *Aparajito* and *The World of Apu* are brilliant representations of Indian life. What makes Ray so accessible to western audiences is his command of film technique and his control of the narrative and acting in his films. Other distinguished films he made

include *The Music Room*, *Company Limited*, *Distant Thunder*, *The Middleman*, *The Chess Players* and *Days and Nights in the Forest*. Ray could be described as rather a "literary" director in that his films are often adaptations of novels, strong on plot and character, but he also had a genuine instinct for what can hold an audience in the cinema. He is probably the only Indian movie director to achieve lasting international fame; certainly the *Apu* trilogy is a fine achievement.

ABOVE *Satyajit Ray's movies often examined the underlying corruption in Indian society.* The Middleman *was one of his best films.*

BELOW *Spanish director Pedro Almodóvar directs Joaquin Cortes and Marisa Paredes in* The Flower of My Secret *(1995), which explores the breakdown of a woman writer. Almodóvar's movies inhabit borderline territory between art movies and exploitative commercial fare. He won a Best Original Screenplay Oscar for* Talk to Her *(2002), which he wrote and directed.*

THE MOVIE WORLD

T HERE IS reality and there are movies.
Only occasionally do the two converge.
American movies, in particular, have always
specialized in the creation of an "unreality",
a never-never land, a dream world intended to
distract the mass audience from what is perceived
as the humdrum facts of their lives. If that sounds
patronizing, then that is what Hollywood often
does to its audience. In this section, we look at
the world that the movies create and the world
that the industry itself inhabits.

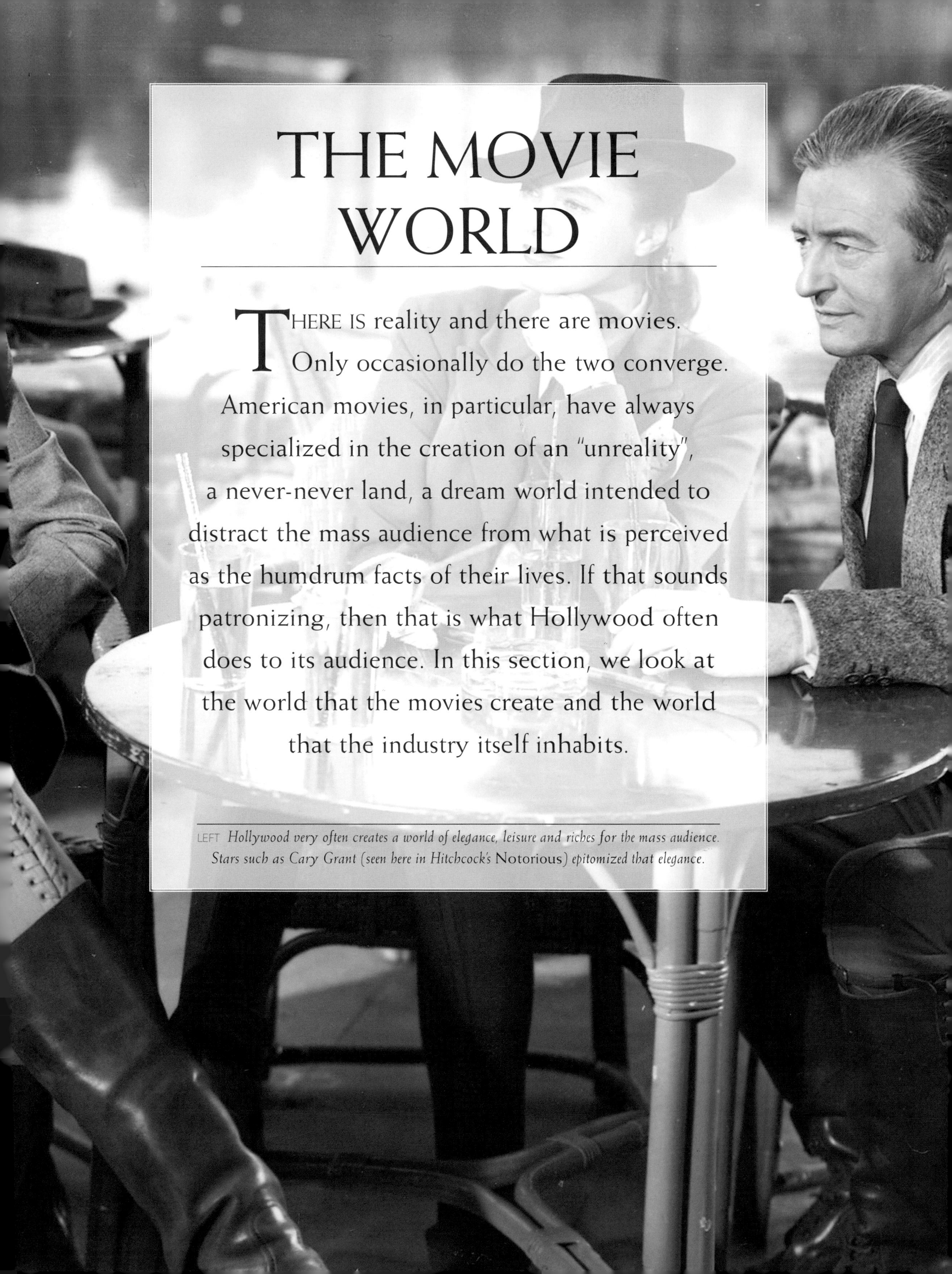

LEFT *Hollywood very often creates a world of elegance, leisure and riches for the mass audience.*
Stars such as Cary Grant (seen here in Hitchcock's Notorious*) epitomized that elegance.*

INTRODUCTION

In his excellent book, *America in the Dark*, David Thomson writes about "Hollywood and the gift of unreality". His argument is that Hollywood created a separate reality, indeed an alternative reality, which obeyed different rules from that of everyday life. The prime function of the movies was to create unreality for the masses. Whenever films did touch on social issues or life as we know it, Hollywood managed to distort the reality of things to provide reassuring messages and resolutions. In life, there may be a few happy endings; in Hollywood, there is almost always a happy ending. Its staple fare is the "feel-good" movie. It sells hope and solace. From Busby Berkeley musicals to Steve Martin comedies, from Bette Davis melo-dramas to gross-out comedies, the message has remained much the same: trust in the American Way of Life and, even though things may appear hopeless, a happy ending will somehow be conjured up for you.

However, not even Hollywood can provide endlessly carefree movies of the Andy Hardy and *Lassie Come Home* variety. There have to be bumpy rides along the way before the uplifting chords of the final reprise of the score usher us out of the cinema to face real life again. You can fool most of the people a lot of the time, but not all of the customers all of the time,

so signs of social conflict or contradictions must be represented in some movies. And that is where genre movies come in: the westerns, the musicals, the gangster movies, the horror flicks, the science fiction epics, the adventure films, the swash-bucklers, the screwball comedies, the war pictures, the epics and the social issue movies.

Genres made commercial sense because the studios could sell an easily identifiable product to a mass audience accustomed to buying that product. However, genre movies were also a useful means of representing a conflict within society, often between an individual and the community, and of reaching a compromise resolution

that reinforced the values of the community. Thus, a western such as *Shane* (1953) could show the conflict between a greedy rancher and small homesteaders, and resolve the conflict through the figure of Shane, the buckskin-clad, loner hero (Alan Ladd), who has to move on when, through his special skills as a gunman,

LEFT AND BELOW *Biopics were a staple genre of all the major studios. Examples include the Cary Grant movie* Night and Day, *supposedly about the life of Cole Porter (below), and* Rommel, Desert Fox, *starring James Mason as the German World War II general (left).*

he has made the valley safe for the homesteaders to grow their families and crops. Message: you need a professional, specially skilled military person to defend the rights of ordinary citizens against bullies of one kind or another (perhaps a particularly useful message for the Cold War era).

Courtroom dramas are almost a separate genre of their own; in *12 Angry Men* Henry Fonda played the

ABOVE *Greta Garbo became a major asset for the industry in the 1930s, starring in lavish MGM productions such as* Marie Walewska.

ABOVE The Big Clock (1948) starred Charles Laughton and Ray Milland and was an example of film noir, which was granted genre status by movie critics.

classic role of the liberal in the cream suit who gently persuaded his fellow jurors that they were wrong to find a Hispanic youth guilty of murder, thereby condemning him to the electric chair. In the movie, all the conflicts and dissensions among the jury members are smoothed over and the American system of justice is triumphantly vindicated by the end of the film. The issue of the rights and wrongs of capital punishment is not even addressed. However, the

ABOVE Disaster movies keep getting made; witness the recent Titanic. One of the most successful disaster movies at the box office was the 1974 The Towering Inferno.

audience feels reassured by the proceedings and, indeed, grateful to such a wonderful judicial system and leaves the cinema with the thought that there will always be a Henry Fonda around to prevent injustice. Oh, yeah? Well, it only happens in the world of the movies, that world of unreality.

Hollywood, someone once said, is a state of mind rather than a place. However, it is a place as well, although only one studio, Paramount, now physically remains there. Every year the workers and executives of this mythical or real place, depending on your point of view, come together to present prizes to one another in the

Oscars ceremony. As usual with Hollywood, the business end of things is the driving force behind the hype of this orgy of congratulation.

The Oscars achieve massive publicity for the American film industry, and the winning actors and directors find that their value in the market place has increased considerably. However, the publicity that Hollywood courts and actively co-operates with also has its down side, and that is the possibility of scandal. The publicity hounds who eat up Hollywood hype can also bite the hands that feed them, and many a star or film personality has succumbed

ABOVE Errol Flynn acts out a scene with his co-stars during the shooting of the 1939 western Dodge City.

to the pressures of living their lives in the endless limelight of fame. Hollywood may try to arrange itself and its movies to convey a rosy and wholesome image, but occasionally Superman is found without his cape on and looks like a sleazy creature from the sewers.

LEFT Irwin Allen's The Day the World Ended starred important Hollywood stars like Paul Newman and William Holden, but the stars and script played second fiddle to the special effects of the disaster genre.

BELOW David Cronenberg is sometimes called the thinking man's horror movie director. This 1987 remake of the 1950s Vincent Price version of The Fly starred Jeff Goldblum as the guy who turns into a fly.

85

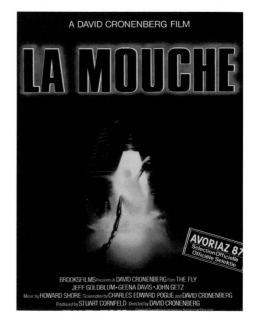

THE SILENT YEARS

Irving Thalberg is quoted as saying there never was any such thing as a silent movie. He described how at MGM in the pre-sound days he would sit with other executives in the screening room and watch MGM's latest offering in despair at what he saw, wondering what kind of product they had to sell to the public. Then they would put the movie into a cinema, either with a fully fledged orchestra or pianist to provide musical accompaniment, and suddenly there was drama, excitement and magic on the screen. The music did more than simply underscore the narrative the audience was seeing; it told them what to feel and how to react. When we talk about "the silents" we should always bear Thalberg's dictum in mind. Indeed, when silents are revived now for theatrical showings, they usually have an added soundtrack of specially written music.

However, when Georges Méliès, theatre owner in Paris at the end of the 19th century, began making films,

ABOVE *Georges Méliès dealt in cinematic magic, as this shot of the moon getting one in the eye demonstrates. 2001 it isn't, but to turn-of-the-century audiences coming fresh to this new art, this was spectacle indeed.*

musical accompaniment was not part of his plans. He merely saw film as an extension of his skill as an illusionist. But the movies he made caught on, and in 1900 he filmed the story of Cinderella. Along the way he discovered the use of fades and dissolves, slow (and fast) motion and animation, especially in his science fiction films *A Trip to the Moon* and *An Impossible Voyage.* The first real "movie" is generally reckoned to be

The Great Train Robbery. It was made by Edwin Porter, one of a group of American pioneers who were inspired by the likes of Méliès to use the new invention as a means of narrative. Porter's films became regular features in the fare served up to audiences by the nickelodeons.

In the beginning, films were photographed with a stationary camera, which recorded what happened in front of it in an unbroken sequence. Movies did not seem all that different from stage plays, except that the actors were not actually performing there in the theatre. Close-ups and editing techniques were slow to come, until Griffith got to work moving the technique of the motion picture towards what we recognize as the art of the cinema nowadays. His use of close-ups, editing techniques, cross-cutting and composition within the frame was to reach its apotheosis in *The Birth of a Nation.* The cinema would never be the same again.

THE CREATION OF STARS

The actors who appeared in those early movies were largely anonymous, until a certain Florence Lawrence broke the barrier because of her popularity with audiences. She became known as "The Biograph Girl" – a star had been born and producers

began to realize that you could sell movies by association with big names. Famous stars would provide what the producers desperately needed – "product identification" – and competition for the hottest new properties increased dramatically. Mary Pickford, for example, who joined Biograph in 1909, became a favourite of the masses, was dubbed "America's Sweetheart", and ended up earning more than half-a-million dollars a year from Paramount.

LEFT *One of the top female stars of the silent era was Lilian Gish, who was in Griffith's* The Birth of a Nation *(1915).*

Movies were now attracting famous stars from the stage and vaudeville, including John Barrymore, Walter Hampden, Gaby Deslys the opera star, Geraldine Farrar and W.C. Fields. Mary Pickford was the highest-paid, but sweetness was not the only draw: Theda Bara became the first screen "vamp", a female who devoured men. Charlie Chaplin also shot to fame from a debut in a Keystone comedy; he was shortly signed by the Essanay company for 1250 dollars a week. Douglas Fairbanks became an instant star with his first film, *The Lamb,* and William S. Hart was the first screen western hero.

SILENT COMEDY

What most people remember from the silent years are the comedies: the Mack Sennett Keystone Kops series, Charlie Chaplin, Buster Keaton, Fatty Arbuckle, Harold Lloyd, Ben Turpin and Laurel and Hardy.

Sennett's comedies comprised mad chases, wild mayhem and surreal slapstick involving violence that never seemed to hurt anyone. Indeed, these movies resembled crazy, out-of-control dream sequences where everyday stability was turned upside down. Their function was eventually taken over by cartoons. By way of contrast, the slapstick in Chaplin's silent comedies was minimized. His main talents were as a mime and a kind of comic ballet dancer. His character as the "little tramp" or vagabond was milked for every drop of pathos. The other great comedian of the 1920s, Buster Keaton, was less interested in making his audiences feel sorry for the incompetents and unfortunates he impersonated, and instead specialized in amazing stunts and acrobatics. All the same, "Old Stoneface" as he was known, gained the audience's sympathy by more subtle means.

ABOVE *Florence Lawrence (1886–1938) was known as "The Biograph Girl" and was one of the first stars of silent movies.*

ABOVE *Mary Pickford (1892–1979) was "America's Sweetheart". She and Douglas Fairbanks were Hollywood's first golden couple.*

Fatty Arbuckle was nearly as big a star as Chaplin at the time of his downfall. Harold Lloyd made a living out of appearing to hang out of tall buildings, whilst Ben Turpin's cross-eyed comedian act made up in gusto for what it lacked in comic nuance. Many people see Laurel and Hardy as effectively silent comedians, and among the very greatest of them. Even though most of their films were talkies, they were still basically visual comedians.

Nothing dates faster than comedy, but many of these silent comedies and actors stand the test of time, principally because they are silent. Perhaps visual comedy is more timeless than comedy that depends on dialogue or the witty one-liner. At any rate, television regularly shows compilations of the best sequences from the Hollywood silent comedies, and the sales of videos of some of the best of the silent comedies reflect a continuing public interest. It is interesting to note that only silent comedies made by Hollywood survive to this day. No other national cinema ever rivalled the American film industry in making the world laugh at the antics of these mute lunatics on the screen.

LEFT *Theda Bara (1885–1955) may seem faintly ridiculous now, but in her heyday she was known as the Vamp.*

ABOVE *The Big Four who established United Artists: Douglas Fairbanks, Mary Pickford, Charles Chaplin and D.W. Griffith.*

THE EUROPEANS

When it came to artistic advances, the real progress was taking place in Europe, particularly in Germany, Russia, France and

ABOVE *Louise Brooks, one of the great silent stars, appeared in German director G.W. Pabst's* Pandora's Box *(1929). But her career did not survive long into the sound era.*

Scandinavia. In Germany the Expressionist movement strongly influenced directors such as Fritz Lang in *Die Niebelungen* (1924), *Metropolis* (1927) and *Spies* (1928). Similarly, Robert Wiene's *The Cabinet of Dr Caligari* (1919) showed the influence of Cubist painting. F.W. Murnau, another distinguished German director, made important films in *The Last Laugh* (1924) and *Faust* (1926).

In Russia, the leaders of the Revolution soon realized the propaganda value of the infant medium. Sergei Eisenstein became the most famous director in the world, and an important film theoretician as well.

ABOVE *A famous shot from Eisentein's* The Battleship Potemkin *(1925).*

His films, *Strike* (1924), *The Battleship Potemkin* (1925) and *October* (1928), reflected his belief in the power of montage sequences – the editing of film in a succession of closely controlled shots to produce a specific effect on the cinema audience.

"A COLLAR BUTTON UNDER A LENS AND THROWN ON A SCREEN MAY BECOME A RADIANT PLANET."
SERGEI EISENSTEIN

In France, Abel Gance produced *Napoléon* (1927), a film shot for multiple projectors throwing images on a triple screen. Jean Renoir, the son of the Impressionist painter, began his long film career with *The Water Girl*

(1924) and *Nana* (1925). In Sweden, Mauritz Stiller made *The Emigrants* (1921), *Gunnar Hedes Saga* (1922) and *The Saga of Gosta Berling* (1924), which launched the film career of a rather chubby young woman, Greta Garbo. In Denmark, Carl Dreyer became known worldwide for his movies *The Parson's Widow* (1920), *Master of the House* (1925) and *The Passion of Joan of Arc* (1928).

RIGHT *Abel Gance was a French director who thought big, and if he had been alive in the 1950s he would have been handed many an epic to direct. Napoléon (1927) ran for six hours and was meant to be one of six films – but the other five were never made. It traces Napoleon's career from a schoolboy to his invasion of Italy in 1797. Napoléon is still regularly revived today – note the "Francis Coppola presents" heading for this re-release.*

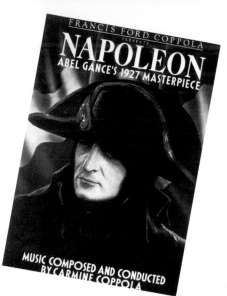

FRANCIS FORD COPPOLA
presents
NAPOLEON
ABEL GANCE'S 1927 MASTERPIECE

MUSIC COMPOSED AND CONDUCTED BY CARMINE COPPOLA

THE SILENT 20s IN HOLLYWOOD

LEFT *Al Jolson initiated sound in the movies in* The Jazz Singer *(1927).*

Hollywood was producing its own masterpieces in the last years of the silents. Erich von Stroheim was a highly extravagant maverick director who eventually found it impossible to operate within the Hollywood system which put such a premium on making a cost-effective product with an assembly-line production method. Before his directorial career was eclipsed, however, he made *Foolish Wives* (1922), *Greed* (1923) and *The Wedding March* (1928). The Swede Victor Sjöström directed Lillian Gish in *The Scarlet Letter* (1926) and *The Wind* (1928). D.W. Griffith directed the melodrama *Broken Blossoms* with Lillian Gish and Richard Barthelmess in 1919, followed by *Way Down East* (1920), *Orphans of the Storm* (1922) and *America* (1924).

The great comedians Chaplin and Keaton helped to give screen comedy a new status. Chaplin with *The Gold Rush* (1925) and *The Circus* (1928), and Keaton with *The Navigator* (1924) and *The General* (1927), earned themselves serious attention as creative artists. Douglas Fairbanks achieved huge success with *The Three Musketeers* (1921), *Robin Hood* (1922), *The Thief of Bagdad* (1924) and *The Black Pirate* (1926), which was a very early exercise in colour film.

Fans who liked their stars larger-than-life adored Rudolph Valentino in *The Sheik* (1921), *Blood and Sand* (1922) and *The Eagle* (1925). Alla Nazimova, starring in *Salome* (1923) and *The Redeeming Sin* (1925), tried her utmost to be exotic and other-worldly enough to satisfy the fantasies of millions of men.

Then on October 6, 1927, the première of *The Jazz Singer* took place. Al Jolson was heard speaking one line: "You ain't heard nothing yet, folks. Listen to this." The sound film was born and two years later silent movies were finished.

BELOW *Zasu Pitts in Erich von Stroheim's silent masterpiece,* Greed. *Stroheim originally shot 50 reels of film but reduced it to a four-hour running time before an exasperated Irving Thalberg cut it to around 100 minutes.*

THE STUDIOS

From the mid-1920s on, Hollywood film production functioned within the studio system. The system established a factory production style, in essence no different from a Ford assembly line except that what rolled off the production line were not automobiles but movies. To the moguls who ran the studios, and the money men who controlled the finances in New York, movies were first and foremost a business.

In fact, the "Big Five" (MGM, Paramount, Fox, Warner Brothers and RKO) had more money invested in real estate than in film production. This real estate was in the form of first-run cinemas in the best positions in the principal cities of America. The studios had to make enough major features to service these cinemas and also the affiliated chains with which they had special agreements. As we have seen, each of the five majors was involved in the three aspects of the movie business: production, distribution and exhibition.

None of the majors made enough top-notch features in a year to service their own cinemas, which normally required weekly changes of programme, so the cinemas they owned showed the products of other studios as well. For example, if MGM had a huge hit on its hands, the other companies would benefit from that success through the box-office returns from the cinemas they owned that showed the MGM movie. The major studios were nominally in competition with one another, but in fact they formed an oligopoly that dominated the American film industry and successfully blocked entry to lesser fry. It would be the late 1940s before the American government would act decisively to force the majors to divest themselves of their exhibition function and thereby end the monopoly that had lasted more than 20 years.

The other large studios, Columbia, Universal and United Artists (the company formed by Pickford, Fairbanks, Chaplin and Griffith) were known as the "Little Three". They were prevented from competing with the five majors because they did not have the control over the exhibition side of the business that the majors wielded. However, they were still big studios capable of producing major films.

In addition, there were the "Poverty Row" outfits such as Republic and Monogram, and independent producers who would hope to sell their product to one of the majors.

By 1919, the American film industry had established a dominant position in the world film markets. It is a position that has never seriously been challenged. American cinema is dominant and that dominance had its foundations in the studio system. Even though that system began to break up in the 1950s, the studios survive in some form to this day, despite the many changes in ownership and function. However, their role has changed completely.

MGM

MGM is probably the most famous of all the Hollywood studios. Its proud boast that it had more stars than there are in heaven typifies the studio's general approach: give the public glamour, gloss and glitz. MGM film-makers had a motto they were meant to subscribe to: "Make it good, make it big, give it class." "Ars Gratia Artis" was the legend that appeared above Leo the Lion, MGM's trademark, which is loosely translated as "Art for art's sake"; but art had nothing to do with MGM movies if Louis B. Mayer had anything to do with it. The mogul who ran MGM for 25 years was more interested in providing corny, "family" entertainment to draw the public in.

THE BEGINNINGS

MGM came into being in 1924 with the merger of Metro Pictures, Goldwyn Pictures (minus Sam Goldwyn) and Louis B. Mayer's company. It was the Studio production arm of Loew's Inc., headed by Marcus Loew in New York, which is where all the financial decisions were made.

Louis B. Mayer and the "boy wonder" Irving Thalberg were in charge of production at Culver City, the home of MGM. From the start they put their faith in stars and in top technicians. Curiously, MGM was never a particularly happy hunting-ground for directors: the studio's producers and the heads of the various technical departments were more powerful. Their main task was to create showcases for the glamorous stars MGM took enormous trouble to groom and market. Thalberg would work very closely with his producers and with the writers to produce vehicles for these stars, and only when they had the "product" right did they assign a director to a picture.

1925–1940

Two silent hits for MGM were the 1925 version of *Ben-Hur*, with Ramon Navarro, and King Vidor's *The Big Parade*, a war movie of the same year. The 1929 musical *The Broadway Melody* was the first talking picture to make big bucks for the studio. Garbo was an MGM star, and she starred in her first sound film *Anna Christie* in

ABOVE *British star Robert Donat starred with Greer Garson in the classic MGM movie* Goodbye, Mr Chips (1939). *This was Garson's film debut.*

1930, and in 1932 *Grand Hotel* featured a roster of MGM luminaries: Lionel Barrymore, Joan Crawford, John Barrymore and Wallace Beery. The latter, along with child star Jackie Cooper, also made audiences weep in the aisles in *The Champ* (1931).

The "look" of MGM films was glossy – "stars shot through cellophane wrapping" – but two of their most popular stars in the 1930s went against the house style: Wallace Beery and Marie Dressler. Garbo was the ultimate ethereal star and MGM exploited her in *Queen Christina* (1933) and *Camille* (1936), with Robert Taylor as Armand. Two other major stars emerged in the 1930s: Clark Gable and Joan Crawford. These two were teamed together in eight movies, almost all of them entirely forgettable.

LEFT *Greer Garson was groomed by MGM to be the "great lady" of the screen. She was meant to represent class and gentility among a galaxy of stars that MGM was constantly boasting about.*

ABOVE *"Make it big!" was part of MGM's credo, and they didn't come any bigger in the 1940s than David Selznick's production of* Gone with the Wind.

Gable made a lot of money for the studio in *Mutiny on the Bounty* (1935), with Charles Laughton as Captain Bligh going well over the top, and in *San Francisco* (1936). The decade ended with the première of *Gone with the Wind* (1939), which David Selznick produced for MGM.

1940–1960

MGM had found a gold mine in the series of Andy Hardy pictures they had started in the late 1930s, featuring Mickey Rooney. The family entertainment these movies offered (and their endorsement of American small-town values) warmed Louis B. Mayer's heart and filled Loew's coffers. Under producer Arthur Freed, the Freed Unit at MGM produced a series of "teenage musicals" with Mickey Rooney and Judy Garland, and then graduated to elaborate technicolor

RIGHT *Hurd Hadfield on the set of* The Picture of Dorian Gray, *the 1945 MGM adaptation of Oscar Wilde's novel. MGM prided itself on its "classy" products and often adapted literary works for the screen.*

musicals that created new standards for the genre: *Meet Me in St Louis* (1944), *On the Town* (1949), *An American in Paris* (1951), *Singin' in the Rain* (1952) and *The Band Wagon*

(1953). MGM's musical stars were the best in the business: Gene Kelly, Fred Astaire, Judy Garland and Cyd Charisse. They also employed the most talented directors of musicals: Vincente Minnelli, Gene Kelly, Stanley Donen and Charles Walters.

However, musicals were expensive to produce and did not bring great returns on investment during a period in which MGM badly needed an upturn in its profits. In 1951 Mayer was replaced as head of production by Dore Schary, but the more radical and adventurous former RKO man did not manage to halt MGM's downward slide, although *Quo Vadis?* (1951), *Cat on a Hot Tin Roof* (1958), *Gigi* (1958) and *Ben-Hur* (1959) all did well for the studio. By then, musicals, MGM's pride, were going out of fashion and they had become too expensive to make anyway.

RIGHT *MGM musicals were the pride of the studio. Most of the best musicals, such as* Singin' in the Rain, *were produced by the Freed Unit under the supervision of producer Arthur Freed.*

1960 ONWARDS

In the mid-1960s MGM had a few good years, based on the box-office returns of some major hits: *How the West was Won* (1962), *Doctor Zhivago* (1965), *The Dirty Dozen* (1967) and *2001* (1968). The early 1970s saw new owners selling off backlots and studio props and cutting back to four or five movies a year, but the studio had recovered sufficiently by the early 80s to be able to purchase United Artists after the debacle of *Heaven's Gate* helped to ruin the studio. In 1986 Ted Turner, at that time the owner of the CNN television news channel, bought MGM/UA. One attraction for Turner was that he was

able to buy the MGM and United Artists film library; thus the Turner Classic Movies television channel (TCM) had an Aladdin's Cave of film goodies to source it. Since then, the ownership of MGM/UA has changed hands several times; it is still in the movie-making business but the great days of Gable, Garbo, Kelly, Astaire, Tracy and Hepburn are gone forever.

The doyen of the studio system at its zenith, MGM produced the most wish-fulfilling of all the fantasies of the dream factory.

BELOW *By the 1980s MGM imported most of the films they gave their name to, like this 1988 George Lucas production* Willow, *which starred Val Kilmer and Joanne Whalley. It did not wow the box office.*

PARAMOUNT

Paramount was born in 1916 from the merging of Adolph Zukor's Famous Players Film Company with Jesse Lasky's company and the Paramount distribution company. Zukor would become one of Hollywood's most hard-nosed moguls, building the empire that would eventually make Paramount Hollywood's biggest studio. As a businessman he realized that you could only play in the ballpark if you were heavily involved in the three major aspects of the film business: production, distribution and exhibition. Thus Paramount, like the other four majors, became a vertically integrated business that wielded enormous influence in the film market.

1916–1929

Zukor set great store by star names, as is evidenced by the name of his first company: Famous Players. Among the stars he had in the early years were Douglas Fairbanks, Mary Pickford, Wallace Reid, Billie Burke and William S. Hart. In the 1920s Valentino made huge profits for the studio in *The Sheik* and *Blood and Sand*. Cecil B. De Mille directed his first version of *The Ten Commandments* in 1923, whilst Ronald Colman made an early version of *Beau Geste* in 1926. *The Covered Wagon* in 1923 was the first epic western. *Wings* (1927) was a spectacular "flying" movie set in World War I.

THE 1930S

Paramount in the 1930s was the studio where the Marx Brothers, Mae West and W.C. Fields exploited their particular forms of comic mayhem. The western was also one of Paramount's favourite genres: the laconic Gary Cooper starred in *The Plainsman* (1936) whilst Joel McCrea strapped on the gun holsters for *Wells Fargo* in 1937. De Mille donned his religious hat to direct *The Sign of the Cross* (1932) and *The Crusades* (1935), and in between these efforts he miscast Claudette Colbert as *Cleopatra* in 1934. Prestige productions came in the form of Preston Sturges's comedies, Frank Borzage's *A Farewell to Arms* (1932) starring Gary Cooper and Helen Hayes, and the exotic fantasies

ABOVE *These are the famous Paramount Pictures gates, through which all hopefuls had to pass if they wanted to make it with the studio. Some never got past the gatemen.*

dreamed up by Josef von Sternberg for Marlene Dietrich: *Morocco* (1930), *Shanghai Express* (1932) and *The Scarlet Empress* (1934). But it was in the musical field that Paramount really

ABOVE *Paramount was appalled with the Austrian's director's extravagance in movies such as* Greed *and* Queen Kelly. *Von Stroheim was never allowed to direct a movie in the sound era.*

ABOVE *Cecil B. De Mille was one of Paramount's most successful directors. His religious epics netted the studio huge profits over the years, with their queasy mixture of religiosity and sex.*

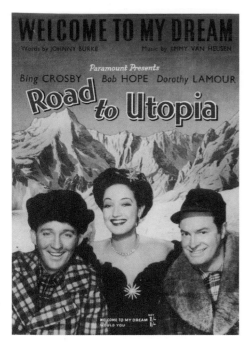

ABOVE *Crosby, Hope and Lamour spelled box-office riches for Paramount in the series of* Road *movies.*

competed. Jeanette MacDonald starred with Maurice Chevalier in three musicals, including the delightful *Love Me Tonight* directed by Rouben Mamoulian. Bing Crosby was a major Paramount star, as were Bob Hope, Betty Grable, George Raft and Dorothy Lamour.

1940–1960

With their series of *Road* pictures, Hope and Crosby boosted Paramount profits enormously in the 1940s and 50s. Other major Paramount stars were Alan Ladd with *This Gun for Hire, The Glass Key* and *The Blue Dahlia*. Victor Mature and Hedy Lamarr wooed the audiences away from their television sets in 1949 with

"AN EXECUTIVE CANNOT EXPECT LOVE – EVER!"
DARRYL ZANUCK

Samson and Delilah, while Bing Crosby and Barry Fitzgerald did a good P.R. job for the Catholic church in *Going My Way*. Without Crosby, Hope made big bucks with *The Paleface* and *Son of Paleface*. An all-star cast including James Stewart and Betty Hutton made De Mille's *The Greatest Show on Earth* (1952) a huge success. Alan Ladd had the greatest role of his career in the 1953 *Shane*, whilst De Mille could not avoid preaching again in the extremely vulgar *The Ten Commandments* of 1956 with Charlton Heston as Moses parting the Red Sea. Critical plaudits as well as box-office success came with Hitchcock's *Rear Window* (1954), starring James Stewart with Grace

ABOVE *A box-office winner for Paramount was Danny Kaye in a series of inventive comedies. Here he is with Glynis Johns in* The Court Jester (1956), *in which he explains, "The pellet with the poison's in the vessel with the pestle, the chalice from the palace has the brew that is true."*

Kelly, and *Psycho* in 1960. Among famous directors who worked at Paramount during this period were Billy Wilder (*The Lost Weekend* and *Sunset Boulevard*), Preston Sturges (*The Miracle of Morgan's Creek*, *Hail the Conquering Hero*) and William Wyler (*The Heiress*).

THE 1960S ONWARDS

The Carpetbaggers (1964) gave Paramount a hit movie and the studio also did very well with *Rosemary's Baby* (1968), directed by Roman Polanski, and the glutinous *Love Story* in 1970. However, it really hit the jackpot in 1972 with *The Godfather*, directed by Francis Coppola. *The Godfather Part II* also did well in 1974, but not on the scale of *Saturday Night Fever* (1977) and *Grease* (1978), both starring John Travolta. These box-office receipts were eclipsed in the 1980s by the Indiana Jones movies *Raiders of the Lost Ark* and *Indiana Jones and the Temple of Doom*. Eddie Murphy arrived as a major star in *Beverly Hills Cop* and Paul Hogan surprised the studio by making it a lot of money with *Crocodile Dundee*. Other hits included *Top Gun*, *Terms of Endearment*, *Trading Places*, the *Star Trek* movies and *An Officer and a Gentleman*.

ABOVE *Robert Evans was the golden boy of the Paramount production executives in the 1970s, helping to bring to the screen the* Godfather *movies and* Chinatown. *His fall from grace was spectacular, however, and his career never recovered.*

PARAMOUNT NOW

In 1966 Gulf & Western took over Paramount. The days of Adolph Zukor and the great movie entrepreneurs were long gone. Paramount became part of a much larger company that had had no previous experience in the film industry. In 1993 Paramount was bought by the conglomerate Viacom. The studio has continued to have its successes and seems set to remain a major presence in the industry for as long as movies survive.

ABOVE *Rosemary's Baby, directed by Roman Polanski and starring Mia Farrow, was a huge hit for Paramount in 1968.*

ABOVE *Grease (1978) was a major box-office hit for Paramount. It starred John Travolta and Olivia Newton-John. With* Saturday Night Fever *and this hit, Travolta's career was riding high.*

20th CENTURY FOX

William Fox began in nickelodeons, then built picture palaces, moved into film distribution and finally production. He was one of the entrepreneurs who challenged the monopoly of the Motion Picture Patents Company. Fox's first film was made in 1914 (*Life's Shop Window*), but it was the emergence of Theda Bara as a major star that helped establish the Fox Film Company. In the mid-1920s Fox managed to acquire cinemas in prime sites and strengthened the company's position in relation to its main rivals.

However, hard times followed when the stock-market crash of 1929 hit the company; Fox was forced to sell his shares. Five years later Fox merged with 20th Century Pictures under Darryl Zanuck and Joseph Schenck: 20th Century Fox was created.

THE PRE-1940 FOX MOVIES

What Price Glory?, *Sunrise* and *Seventh Heaven* were three of the more memorable Fox silents. Janet Gaynor was the studio's top silent star, and she was joined in the 1930s by Spencer Tracy (until he went to MGM), Warner Baxter, Will Rogers, Alice Faye, Sonja Henie, Don

ABOVE *Tyrone Power was a major star for Fox for many years.* The Razor's Edge *(1946) was Fox's film version of the Somerset Maugham novel.*

Ameche, Tyrone Power and the biggest box-office attraction of them all, Shirley Temple. *Little Miss Marker* (1934), *The Littlest Rebel* (1935), *Dimples* (1936), *Wee Willie Winkie* (1937), *Rebecca of Sunnybrook Farm* (1938), *The Little Princess* (1939) and several others starring the diminutive but resistible moppet, made Fox big money: she was the envy of other moguls, including Louis B. Mayer at MGM, who, according to Judy Garland, was obsessed with Temple. Alice Faye, Don Ameche and Sonja Henie were the musical stars, and Tyrone Power was the romantic leading man in *In Old Chicago*, *Alexander's Ragtime Band*,

ABOVE *Tyrone Power, Ava Gardner, Mel Ferrer, Errol Flynn and Eddie Albert starred in this 1957 Fox film version of Hemingway's novel* The Sun Also Rises.

Rose of Washington Square, The Rains Came and Jesse James. John Ford directed Henry Fonda in Drums Along the Mohawk in 1939.

1940 ONWARDS

The 1940s started auspiciously for Fox with John Ford's adaptation of Steinbeck's The Grapes of Wrath, and The Oxbow Incident, directed by William Wellmann. Betty Grable and Carmen Miranda starred in a series of brash musicals whilst Jennifer Jones attempted to raise the tone somewhat in The Song of Bernadette (1943). Clifton Webb was a huge hit in Cheaper by the Dozen and Olivia de Havilland suffered in The Snake Pit (1948). Cary Grant and Ann Sheridan sparred in I Was a Male War Bride. In the 1950s, with a decrease in audiences hitting Hollywood, Fox led the industry in

CLEOPATRA

ABOVE Cleopatra, the 1962 Taylor–Burton version, was so expensive to make that it nearly bankrupted the studio and scarcely made its money back at the box office.

introducing CinemaScope with The Robe (1953). They now had Marilyn Monroe as a star, and she helped make How to Marry a Millionaire, Gentlemen Prefer Blondes (both 1953) and The Seven Year Itch (1955) successful. Film versions of stage musicals such as South Pacific and The King and I featured in the 1950s. In the early 60s Fox had a major disaster with the 38-million-dollar Cleopatra starring Elizabeth Taylor. Fox's finances were helped hugely, however, by the stupendous success of The Sound of Music (1965). Butch Cassidy and the Sundance Kid (1969), M*A*S*H (1970) and Patton (1970) with George C. Scott were also hits.

The Star Wars series brought Fox enormous box-office returns in the late 1970s and early 80s, as did the Damien trilogy, starting with The Omen (1976). Alien and Aliens, with new star Sigourney Weaver, did well

LEFT Marilyn Monroe had an ongoing stormy relationship with the Fox studio. Here she starred with Lauren Bacall and Betty Grable in a very successful musical comedy, How to Marry a Millionaire.

ABOVE *The original* Planet of the Apes *series ran to five movies. The first of the series (1968) was by far the best of them, and very much better than the 2001 remake.*

RIGHT **Wall Street,** *directed by Oliver Stone and starring Michael Douglas as Gordon "Greed is good" Gekko, was a prodigious hit for Fox in 1987.*

but were surpassed at the box office by the truly awful *Porky's* series. However, times were rocky for the studio by this time and, as if to prove it, Rupert Murdoch was able to purchase it in 1985. Fox had become part of the conglomerate News International, just another arm of a vast media-owning multinational.

WARNER BROTHERS

There were four Warner brothers: Albert, Harry, Sam and Jack. The whole family helped run a nickelodeon, then the brothers branched out into distribution. Soon they were into production and Warner Bros. came into being in 1923. Among their first successes were the *Rin Tin Tin* movies starring a lovable dog, while Ernst Lubitsch, a director of sharp comedies, gave the studio's productions some tone during the silent years. It was Warners' *The Jazz Singer* and its huge success that revolutionized Hollywood. Warner Bros. had truly arrived.

WARNER BROTHERS AND THE DEPRESSION

Warners attempted to build on the success of the Al Jolson movie with a number of musicals, but the public soon tired of this fare. Warners then turned to gangsters and social realism, and if there is one studio associated with the Depression and the New Deal, it is surely this one. Whereas MGM and Mayer were associated with a devout Republicanism, the Warner brothers were more sympathetic to the Democratic president, Roosevelt. Criticism of a society indifferent to poverty and hardship was implicit in the movies that starred Edward G. Robinson, James Cagney and Paul Muni. Movies such as *Little Caesar, I Am a Fugitive from a Chain Gang* and *The Public Enemy* reflected the underside of the American Dream and made criminals anti-heroes. Then the studio's products changed course, partly due to condemnation from official sources and pressure groups. In 1933 Busby Berkeley made three musicals for the Depression, *42nd Street* (directed by Lloyd Bacon), *Gold Diggers of 1933* and *Footlight Parade.* They offered audiences eroticism and spectacle whilst acknowledging in passing the reality of poverty and deprivation in contemporary America.

Errol Flynn was a major Warners star in the 1930s and 40s with movies such as *Captain Blood* (1935), *The Adventures of Robin Hood* (1938) and

ABOVE *Errol Flynn starred in this 1938 Warner Brothers production of* The Adventures of Robin Hood, *directed by Michael Curtiz. The movie was a huge hit for Warners and Flynn, and is a fine example of a Hollywood action movie.*

The Sea Hawk (1940). Paul Muni scored in *The Story of Louis Pasteur* (1936), *The Good Earth* (1937), *The Life of Emile Zola* (1937) and *Juarez* (1939). Bette Davis became a major star in *Of Human Bondage* (1935), *Jezebel* (1938), *Dark Victory* (1939), *The Old Maid* (1939) *The Private Lives of Elizabeth and Essex* (1939), *The Letter* (1940), *The Great Lie* (1941), *The Little Foxes* (1942), *Now Voyager* (1942) and *Old Acquaintance* (1943). She was the undisputed queen of the melodramas.

LEFT *James Cagney was a big Warners star in the 1930s. Here he is with Frank McHugh in* The Roaring Twenties (1939), *a typical gangster story about the Prohibition Era.*

ABOVE *Warners stars were expected to do their part in publicizing the studio's movies. Here Errol Flynn, Humphrey Bogart and Gilbert Roland board the "Dodge City Special" (probably unwillingly) to publicize the western* Dodge City *(1939).*

Warners returned to its "social conscience" style with the 1939 *Confessions of a Nazi Spy* with Edward G. Robinson, which was clearly anti-American isolationist in intent.

FROM PEARL HARBOR ON

With America's entry into the war, Warners rallied to the flag with stirring, patriotic movies such as *Sergeant York* (1941), *Yankee Doodle Dandy*, *Across the Pacific* and *Casablanca* (all 1942). The last of these became one of the most famous cult pictures ever shot and made Humphrey Bogart a major star, while doing no harm to the career of Ingrid Bergman. Bogart went on to star in *The Maltese Falcon* (1941), *To Have and Have Not* (1945, with his future wife, Lauren Bacall), *The Big Sleep* (1946) and *The Treasure of the Sierra Madre* (1948). Meanwhile, Joan Crawford had moved over to Warners from MGM, leaving her glamour-girl persona behind her and settling for maternal roles. She shone

in *Mildred Pierce* (1945), *Humoresque* (1946) and *Possessed* (1947), suffering dramatically at the hands of husbands, lovers and children.

Alfred Hitchcock made three movies for the studio: *Rope* (1948), *Under Capricorn* (1949) and *Dial M for Murder* (1954). Judy Garland made her "comeback" film for Warners, *A Star is Born* (1954), whilst director Elia Kazan made James Dean a star in *East of Eden*. Nicholas Ray used Dean again in *Rebel Without a Cause* (1955) and George Stevens directed the new star in Dean's last picture, *Giant* (1956), before he was killed in a car crash. In the 1960s the studio scored with *Who's Afraid of Virginia Woolf?* (1966), *Bonnie and Clyde* (1967), and *Bullitt* (1968). Its production of *My Fair Lady* (1964), however, failed to make the impact expected of it.

A demonic thriller, *The Exorcist* (1973), and the first *Superman* movie (1978) made big profits in the 1970s, as did the disaster movie *The Towering Inferno* (1974). Clint Eastwood did well with *Every Which Way But Loose* (1978) and *Any Which Way You Can* (1980), and Barbra Streisand and Kris Kristofferson helped make the third version of *A Star is Born* (1976) a major hit. The story of the uncovering of the Watergate scandals gave Alan Pakula, the director, and Dustin Hoffman and Robert Redford, the stars, opportunities to shine in *All the President's Men* (1976), whilst Streisand again and Ryan O'Neal helped make *What's Up, Doc?* (1972) a success. In the 1980s Steven Spielberg's influence on *Gremlins* (1984) and *The Goonies* (1985) helped create hits. The follow-up *Superman* movies did well at the box office, as did the dire series of *Police Academy* movies.

WARNER BROTHERS TODAY

In 1989 Time Inc. bought Warners and formed Time Warner. In 1996 Time Warner ate up the Turner Broadcasting System to become the

ABOVE *Christopher Reeve was a superhero in the first of the Superman series (1978). As with the later Batman (1989) and Dick Tracy (1990), Hollywood believed it could only resurrect comic book heroes if they indulged in affectionate send-up. Reeve's performance as the quick-changing defender of the American Way of Life is in line with the series' tongue-in-cheek quality.*

world's largest media conglomerate. The original Warner brothers have all long vanished from the scene, but the studio's great movies with Bogart, Davis, Crawford, Flynn and Cagney are still favourites with all true cinema lovers.

101

ABOVE *The Lethal Weapon series brought immense rewards at the box office for Warners. Critics were less generous.*

RKO

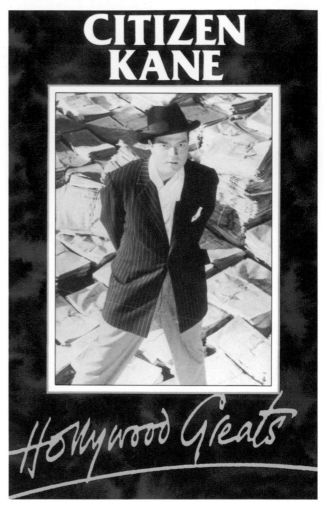

RIGHT *Citizen Kane has repeatedly topped many film critics' lists of the greatest movies of all time.*

RKO is an abbreviation for the Radio-Keith-Orpheum Corporation, which was the result of various mergers between a small movie production and distributing company and the Radio Corporation of America. Hence RKO–Radio Pictures.

David Selznick was an early production chief at the studio and he set himself the difficult task of injecting RKO movies with some quality whilst keeping the budgets very tight. In the 1930s producer Pandro S. Berman made the series of Astaire–Rogers musicals including *Top Hat* (1935), *Swing Time* (1936), *Shall We Dance?* (1937) and *Carefree* (1938). Another famous producer, Merian C. Cooper, produced the classic *King Kong* (1933) which teamed an outsize ape with Fay Wray. Other quality pictures included *Alice Adams* (1935) with Katharine Hepburn and *The Informer* (1935) with Victor McLaglen, directed by John Ford. *The Hunchback of Notre Dame* (1939), directed by William Dieterle and starring Charles Laughton as Quasimodo, also brought critical and commercial success. Even in the 1930s RKO took some commercial risks backing projects whose sure-fire commercial success was not always assured.

RKO was also notable for the number of independent productions it financed. Orson Welles's *Citizen Kane* (1941) and *The Magnificent Ambersons* (1942) were both independent productions which the studio lost money on, but these two movies alone ensured that the RKO name would live on. Yes, RKO executives interfered disastrously with the final cut

ABOVE *King Kong* (1933) *is perhaps, along with* Citizen Kane, *the most famous movie that RKO produced.*

BELOW *RKO, still RKO-Radio at the time of the release of* Sinbad the Sailor (1947), *specialized in small-budget adventure actioners like this swashbuckler that starred Douglas Fairbanks Junior.*

103

ABOVE *Hitchcock made one of his best movies for RKO in 1946,* Notorious, *which starred Cary Grant and Ingrid Bergman. The film was a spy thriller involving a post-war Nazi plot to create an atomic bomb.*

of *The Magnificent Ambersons*, but perhaps the studio should be given some credit for giving Orson Welles his chance in the first place. RKO was the smallest of the Big Five studios, it did not have the financial depth of the other four majors, so this perhaps in part explains why they took more chances with their productions.

During the war, RKO did its bit with John Wayne in *Back to Bataan* (1945) and Gregory Peck as a brave Russian resistance fighter in *Days of Glory* (1944). After the war RKO was one of the leading producers of what came to be known

as *film noir*: *Out of the Past* and *Crossfire*, both released in 1947 and both starring Robert Mitchum, have become noted films of this genre. The movie that brought in the most revenue for the studio, however, was the sickly sweet *The Bells of St Mary's* (1944) with Bing Crosby. Cary Grant and Ingrid Bergman starred in Hitchcock's *Notorious* (1946), but James Stewart in *It's a Wonderful Life* (1947), directed by Frank Capra, failed to attract the expected customers. Now *It's a Wonderful Life* has become everybody's favourite Christmas movie, but in 1947 it rang no bells at the box office.

HOWARD HUGHES ARRIVES

In 1948 Howard Hughes bought the ailing studio and proceeded to indulge his obsessions to the

detriment of the studio's product and finances, although Fritz Lang managed to direct *Rancho Notorious* (1952) and *While the City Sleeps* (1956) at the studio during Hughes's reign. RKO stars in the 1950s included Jane Russell, with whom Hughes was infatuated, Robert Ryan, Jane Greer and Dana Andrews. But too many RKO movies were substandard action and war flicks, and finally Hughes sold out to General Teleradio, who were no better at making successful movies. Finally, in 1958 the studio was sold to Desilu, owned by Lucille Ball and Desi Arnaz, who used it to churn out episodes of *I Love Lucy*. It was a sad ending to the film studio that had made the Astaire–Rogers series, the Orson Welles classics and some of the best of *film noir*.

COLUMNBIA

Founded by brothers Jack and Harry Cohn in 1924, Columbia was for 20 years a comparatively minor studio, partly because it owned no cinemas itself and was therefore squeezed by the majors' monopolistic practices. The 1948 divorcement decree that forced the majors to sell their cinemas helped Columbia establish itself on an equal par with the giants of the industry.

Harry Cohn was the dominant figure in Columbia for many years. Even by the standards set by other movie moguls such as MGM's Louis B. Mayer and Fox's Darryl Zanuck, Cohn was reckoned to be an extremely tough character indeed. Giving no quarter and treating stars, directors and producers alike with total disdain, he brooked no opposition to his rule. He forced female stars such as Rita

RIGHT Gilda starred Rita Hayworth and Glenn Ford in an erotic film noir that played with concepts of sexual identity.

Hayworth to change their appearance to fall in line with what he thought a Columbia star should look like. Generally, Cohn behaved like a medieval autocrat, but he got away with this behaviour because so many people were ambitious to climb the greasy pole of success in Hollywood.

Not that the studio under Harry Cohn did not have its successes: its first great hit was the 1934 *It Happened One Night* with Gable and Colbert. How many times have you seen that clip on television where Gable tries to hitch a lift for Colbert and himself, until Colbert steps forward, hitches her skirt above the knee and brings the traffic screeching to a halt? Yes, movie-goers were easily titillated in those days because the Hays Office imposed such an iron control on what they considered prurient content. Comedy scored again for Columbia in the far superior *Twentieth Century* (1934) with John Barrymore and Carole Lombard. But Columbia was also the studio for cheaply produced series such as the *Blondie* films, serials such as *Batman* and *The Three Stooges* comedy shorts. On a more prestigious level, Jean Arthur and Gary Cooper starred in Frank Capra's *Mr Deeds Goes to Town* (1936). The screwball comedy *His Girl Friday*, with Cary Grant and Rosalind Russell, was a hit in 1940.

Rita Hayworth was the studio's only big star in the 1940s and she made *Cover Girl* with Gene Kelly in 1944 and *Gilda*, the steamy *film noir*,

ABOVE Rita Hayworth as she appeared in the 1948 Columbia production The Lady from Shanghai. *Her then-husband Orson Welles directed the movie.*

with Glenn Ford in 1946. Harry Cohn took a very personal interest in Hayworth, forcing her to undergo painful beauty treatments that altered her appearance quite dramatically. The studio made big bucks with *The Jolson Story* (1946) and *Jolson Sings Again* (1949). In the late 1940s and 50s the studio produced a string of quality pictures: *All the King's Men* (1949), *Born Yesterday* (1950), *From Here to Eternity* (1953), *On the Waterfront* (1954) and *The Bridge on the River Kwai* (1957). Winners for the studio from the 60s and 70s included *A Man for all Seasons* (1966), *Guess Who's Coming to Dinner* (1967), *Funny Girl* (1968) and *Easy Rider* (1969), whilst post-1970,

> "IT'S NOT A BUSINESS,
> IT'S A RACKET."
> *HARRY COHN*
> HEAD OF COLUMBIA

Close Encounters of the Third Kind (1977), *Kramer vs. Kramer* (1979), *Tootsie* (1982), *Ghostbusters* (1984) and *The Karate Kid* series ensured that Columbia stayed in the major league. Columbia was bought by the Coca-Cola company in 1982, then in 1989 Coca-Cola sold the studio to the Sony Corporation. In 1994 Sony reported a financial loss largely due to the poor performance of films made by the Columbia studio. The studio then became part of Sony Pictures Entertainment. The studio founded by the detestable mogul, Harry Cohn, had come a long way from its Poverty Row beginnings.

ABOVE *Columbia won several Oscars with this 1979 production* Kramer vs. Kramer, *which starred Dustin Hoffman and Meryl Streep as parents battling over custody of their son. Some critics saw the movie as a male backlash against feminism.*

BELOW *A big success for Columbia was the 1953 movie* From Here to Eternity. *Here Burt Lancaster and Deborah Kerr are on the beach in the most famous scene of the movie.*

UNIVERSAL

In 1915 Carl Laemmle, the founder of Universal, bought a large piece of land in the Hollywood Hills and named it Universal City. It became a factory for churning out films, very few of which were at all memorable. Erich Von Stroheim, however, made *Foolish Wives* there before Laemmle's general manager, Irving Thalberg, sacked him from his next movie. Irving Thalberg quickly moved on to greater things and became Mayer's right-hand man at MGM. Once Universal studio adapted to sound, they produced *All Quiet on the Western Front* in 1930. This was a rare prestige production in a steady stream of routine dross.

However, the studio was best known for its horror movies and its horror stars, Boris Karloff and Bela Lugosi. *Dracula* (1931), *Frankenstein* (1931), *The Mummy* (1932) and several sequels, *The Bride of Frankenstein* (1935) and *The Invisible Man* series all made profits. In the 1940s the studio's only big money-maker was Claudette Colbert in *The Egg and I* (1947). But in the 50s Universal had big hits with a series of melodramas produced by Ross Hunter and directed by Douglas Sirk: *Magnificent Obsession* (1954), *Written on the Wind* (1956), *The Tarnished Angels* (1958) and *Imitation of Life* (1959). *Winchester 73* (1950) and

ABOVE *Universal was also well known for its horror movies in the 1950s. This was one of the most successful,* The Creature from the Black Lagoon *(1954).*

ABOVE *A 1930 advertisement for the Universal movie* All Quiet on the Western Front, *directed by Lewis Milestone and starring Lew Ayres. The film not only brought an unusual realism to the subject of war but, unlike many other war movies, it also treated German soldiers sympathetically.*

The Glenn Miller Story (1953), both starring James Stewart, also earned money. Anthony Mann made a series of westerns for Universal all starring James Stewart: apart from *Winchester 73* they included *Bend of the River* (1952), *The Naked Spur* (1953), *The Far Country* (1955) and *The Man from Laramie* (1955). Some addicts rate these Anthony Mann-directed Universal-produced westerns among the best ever made.

The studio's roster of stars also included Rock Hudson and Tony Curtis, who starred in westerns and action movies that were churned out for double bills: *The Lawless Breed* (1953), *The Golden Blade* (1953), *Back to God's Country* (1953), *Taza, Son of Cochise* (1954), *Son of Ali Baba* (1952), *The Black Shield of Falworth* (1954) and *The Purple Mask* (1955) were typical. Usually totally forgettable, these films were invariably in

technicolor and had risible scripts, but they brought in the customers in fairly lean times for the industry. A Universal movie of this type will be well-remembered by any film-goers who regularly went to the Odeons or ABCs in the UK in the 1950s. Good value double bills were one of the ways the studios fought against decreasing audiences, and Universal was in the forefront of producing this cheaply-made programme fodder.

However, double bills became a feature of the past and Universal was ready to lose its status as an also-ran in Hollywood. Gradually Universal-International, as it was now known, began climbing into the big league. It was able to employ important stars such as Paul Newman, Burt Lancaster, Steve McQueen and many more, and top directors as well. Its investment in big-budget projects and expensive stars began to pay off. They had a gigantic hit with the 1969 *Butch Cassidy and the Sundance Kid*, which starred Paul Newman as Butch Cassidy and the comparative newcomer Robert Redford as the Sundance Kid. Initially, the studio wanted Steve McQueen for the part, but McQueen wanted top billing over Newman, so Redford was drafted in. His career, and the future of the studio, never looked back.

Universal now entered a period of great success: *Airport* (1970), *The Sting* (1973) and *Jaws* (1975) ensured this. *Jaws* caused the executives at Universal some worries because the costs mounted and stories drifted back to the studio that the mechanical shark around which the movie revolved would not function properly. Executives began to think about replacing the young director Steven Spielberg to whom they had entrusted all this money. But when they saw the finished product, read the reviews and

ABOVE *This double-bill of Universal features from 1952 is typical of the kind of movies Universal produced at this time. Note that this double bill was "to celebrate Universal's 40th anniversary!"*

saw the queues of customers lining up to be scared, then their doubts vanished and they knew they were on to a winner and had discovered a major new directing talent who could deliver critical and commercial success. *Jaws* went on to become one of the all-time biggest money spinners of Hollywood history.

ABOVE **The Sting** *(1973) paired Paul Newman and Robert Redford again in a Universal movie. It was one of the studio's biggest commercial successes.*

ABOVE *Tony Curtis played a Scarlet Pimpernel-type figure in this 1955 Universal swashbuckler,* The Purple Mask.

However, even these box-office successes were eclipsed in the 1980s by Steven Spielberg's *E.T.* (1982) and Robert Zemeckis's *Back to the Future* (1985). *Out of Africa* was another major hit for the studio in 1985. Universal was no longer an also-ran in the Hollywood stakes.

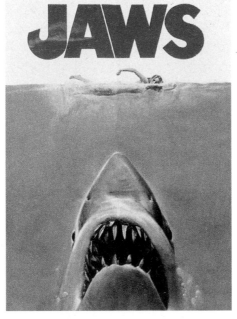

ABOVE *During the shooting of* Jaws *(1975), Universal executives were worried that the young Steven Spielberg was about to ruin the studio; however, the movie made a fortune.*

MCA took over Universal, and ownership of the studio in turn passed to Matsushita, the Japanese conglomerate, which bought the parent company MCA as well. Universal is now a massive presence in film and television production, eating up its rivals. For a long time excluded from the top table in Hollywood, Universal now hands out the invitations and has seen once mighty rivals struggle and even disappear from the scene.

BELOW *An unusual movie for Universal was the 1982* Missing, *which dealt with political events in Chile under a fascist dictatorship. Here, director Costas-Gavras lines up a shot.*

107

UNITED ARTISTS

United Artists was formed by Mary Pickford, Douglas Fairbanks, Charlie Chaplin and D.W. Griffith in 1919 to protect their financial and artistic interests. Griffith left the company in 1924, and his place as a partner was taken by Joseph Schenck, who added some much-needed business acumen. By 1928 the balance sheet was in the black, with Chaplin's *The Circus*, Fairbanks's *The Gaucho* and *The Iron Mask*, and Keaton's *Steamboat Bill Jr* adding to the profits.

In the 1930s the studio produced *The Front Page* (1931), *Les Misérables* and *The Call of the Wild* (both 1935), *Dodsworth* (1936) and *Dead End* (1937). Other memorable pictures included *Stella Dallas* (1937) and *The Prisoner of Zenda* (1937) with Ronald Colman. Laurence Olivier starred in both

RIGHT *The Graduate (1967) introduced Dustin Hoffmann to the screen and made a lot of money for United Artists.*

LEFT *United Artists backed Joseph L. Mankiewicz's movie about Hollywood, the 1954 The Barefoot Contessa, which starred Humphrey Bogart as a burnt-out director and Ava Gardner as a Rita Hayworth-like movie star who marries an aristocrat.*

Wuthering Heights (1939) and *Rebecca* (1940). Alexander Korda, the British producer, was associated with United Artists, making *Things to Come* (1936) and *The Man Who Could Work Miracles* (1937). Westerns included John Ford's classic *Stagecoach* (1939) and the lamentably bad but notorious *The Outlaw*, the Howard Hughes–Jane Russell fiasco, which was made in 1941 but not released until much later.

Chaplin continued to make films for his company: *The Great Dictator* (1940) and *Monsieur Verdoux* (1947). Selznick produced two hit films for UA in the 1940s: the wartime family drama *Since You Went Away* (1944) and

Hitchcock's *Spellbound* (1945). Hard times followed until the early 1950s produced such hits as *The African Queen* (1951) and *High Noon* (1952). Another mega-hit was Mike Todd's *Around the World in Eighty Days* (1956), which made its money from the publicity Todd produced for the movie rather than the quality of the movie itself. By the mid-50s both Chaplin and Pickford had sold their shares in the company. The concept of "the lunatics taking over the running of the asylum" – that is, the artists themselves running a major studio rather than businessmen – had largely been forgotten.

The *Bond* movies, *West Side Story* (1961), *Tom Jones* (1963) and *Midnight Cowboy* (1969) helped make the 1960s a profitable decade for UA, who were taken over in 1967 by the Transamerica Corporation, an insurance conglomerate. Heavy losses were incurred in the early 70s until hits such as *One Flew Over the Cuckoo's Nest* (1975) the *Rocky* series, the *Pink Panther* series and *10* (1979), which starred Bo Derek and Dudley Moore, turned the tide. In the 80s UA continued to finance the *Bond* series and also to profit from *Rocky* and the Stallone persona. Woody Allen is one director/star who makes his movies for

the "new" United Artists. It was MGM that took over United Artists in 1981; thus, the company that was set up to protect artists from the tentacles of the majors at last succumbed to one of the giants of the industry. Ownership of UA has since passed through several hands as the game of Hollywood musical chairs continues.

BELOW *Woody Allen is one director/star who has regularly been funded by United Artists. Here he is seen in his send-up of Tolstoy's* War and Peace, *the 1975* Love and Death.

LEFT *Monogram Pictures was one of the studios located on what was known as Poverty Row in Hollywood because of the cheaply shot quickies they churned out. In this 1944 masterpiece,* The Utah Kid, *the good guy in the orange shirt comes up against a rather elderly sheriff. "B" movie westerns still have their addicts:* The Utah Kid *lives on!*

109

MOVIE GENRES

In the heyday of Hollywood each of the major studios resembled a factory. The aim of these factories was to make a product – movies – that could be shown in cinemas all over the world. The studios had to make enough movies to allow for weekly changes of programme and, at various times in cinematic history, for double-feature bills. When 90 million people in the United States alone were going out to the cinema each week, there seemed to be an unceasing demand for the Hollywood product. To satisfy this demand, movies were produced by a mode of production that was close to an assembly line.

Each worker in that assembly line knew exactly what his or her specific job was. In 1941 a film industry publication calculated that there were 276 separate crafts involved in making a motion picture, and most of those crafts formed guilds that protected their members' right to perform their specific tasks. Studio heads, after their initial misguided opposition to these craft guilds, realized that this kind of "demarcation" philosophy suited their purpose, which was to make the product they required to service their cinemas in sufficient quantity and as cheaply as possible.

"If you've seen one, you've seen 'em all!" is a frequent complaint about the movies, and it is true that movies, certainly in the old days, fell into definite categories, frequently called "genres". Genres made sense economically because a studio could re-use the same sets, locations, actors, directors, costumes and even plots to churn out more westerns, musicals, crazy comedies, war movies, horror flicks, swashbucklers, etc, an assembly line approach which produced economics of scale and which also bred a sense of familiarity in the mass audience. Audiences would know what to expect if they paid their money to see a musical, and if you added Gene Kelly or Judy Garland, then they would have two sets of expectations at least – of the genre and the star. Genres and stars were a means of product differentiation and a way of persuading the customer to come back for more. As a way of producing movies relatively cheaply and encouraging customer loyalty, genre films were good news for the studios. However, talented directors were able to use the generic form to create art.

WESTERNS

The western is the most cinematic of the genres because no other art form can hope to emulate the cinema's power to represent the myths of the American frontier in such an all-embracing manner. But why have westerns been so popular with the public in the past, and why have they largely disappeared from our cinema screens? The answer lies in the way westerns deal in mythology. They present a view of America's frontier and agrarian past that feeds the American Dream: the rugged individual striking out for the unknown, Man against raw Nature, the pursuit of an independent way of life, the acquiring of land and wealth, the conquering of hostile elements in the shape of Indians, and building communities out of the wilderness based on simple values and hard work.

ABOVE *William Boyd as Hopalong Cassidy starred in innumerable "B" westerns and found himself a large fan base especially among the devotees of the Saturday morning Cinema Clubs of the 1940s and 50s.*

ABOVE *William Wellmann's production of* Yellow Sky (1948) *was loosely based on Shakespeare's play* The Tempest, *and starred Gregory Peck and Richard Widmark.*

As the memories of that trail-blazing past recede, the American public may feel less need for frequent doses of western mythology, hence the drastic drop in the number of westerns produced in the last 20 to 30 years. In addition, perhaps too much reality has broken through the mists of legend to sustain the western myths any longer. For example, most Americans now accept that a form of genocide was practised against the Indian population in order for the white man's civilization to flourish. In an era where so-called heroes turn out to be mere mortals after all, it is also difficult to suspend our disbelief when watching these larger-than-life western heroes create law and order out of chaos. Cinema-goers are more interested in the new heroes, the urban guerillas of Jean-Claude Van Damme and Quentin Tarantino movies than the straight-shooting, honest cowboys of yesteryear.

The great days of the western are undoubtedly over. Western fans, however, will debate earnestly which are the truly great westerns: *Stagecoach, My Darling Clementine, Red River, Shane* and *The Searchers* would probably be on most fans' list, although many would speak up for the spaghetti westerns directed by Sergio Leone. Apart from Leone, most western fans would probably rate John Ford, Howard Hawks, Anthony Mann and Clint Eastwood as the top directors of the genre. The western still has life in it, as *The Outlaw Josey Wales, Dances with Wolves* and *Unforgiven* reflect. The western as a genre will never recapture its pre-eminent position, but it will resurface from time to time and still find an audience.

ABOVE The Man Who Shot Liberty Valance (1962) *was one of John Ford's last westerns. It has an elegiac tone as the movie mourns the passing of the old west.*

111

ABOVE *Daniel Day-Lewis starred as Hawkeye in the 1992* The Last of the Mohicans, *directed by Michael Mann.*

MUSICALS

The musical is another genre that Hollywood took over and made its own. When sound came to Hollywood, the studios poured out film after film with people singing and dancing rather inexpertly, and audiences seemed to love these happy films. However, the public soon tired of the new phenomenon – perhaps it was the onset of the Depression, perhaps it was just that there was such a surfeit of musicals.

RIGHT *Fred Astaire and Cyd Charisse starred in the MGM musical* The Band Wagon, *directed by Vincente Minnelli and with a script by Betty Comden and Adolph Green. The plot is a retread of* Singin' in the Rain.

they served up. Berkeley, using the camera to create his elaborate and rather soulless fantasies, was the ace director and choreographer who delivered the goods. Astaire and Rogers had no such truck with reality in their RKO musicals, however; Astaire was debonair and usually rich, Rogers was simply Rogers, the average young woman catapulted into opulent settings and wearing fancy clothes. The black-and-white Art Deco sets, the sumptuous costumes, the vision of society life, the exotic locations – all these elements combined to create pure escapist fantasies for the masses, who were struggling with the realities of unemployment and poverty.

ABOVE *Gene Kelly revolutionized the movie musical in* On the Town (1949), *when he filmed himself and his co-stars Vera Ellen, Frank Sinatra, Betty Garrett, Ann Miller and Jules Munshin singing and dancing against a real New York.*

It took Astaire and Rogers and Busby Berkeley to seduce the customers back into the cinemas to watch musical extravaganzas. Warner Bros., Berkeley's studio, sensed that people needed glamour, hope and extravagance plus an acknowledgement that there were hard times out there, so that's what

ABOVE *After the heyday of the MGM musical, studios invested in only sure-fire hits that had already been proven on stage.* West Side Story (1961) *was one of the more successful transitions of stage musicals to the screen.*

ABOVE *Another stage musical that made it to the big screen was* Hello, Dolly! *(1969) which starred Barbra Streisand.*

Musicals are inherently "utopian" – they concoct an alternative vision of reality that panders to our dreams. The search for love and popularity, success and wealth, is always celebrated in them. Love leads to marriage, putting on a show leads to massive popularity and success, the coupling of boy-and-girl strengthens the community and reinforces role models and orthodoxy. All movie genres are conservative in the values they espouse, and none more so than the musical. In the 1940s and 50s, the heyday of the MGM musical, some more adult elements were introduced to the storylines, but the resolution was always the same: Kelly would win Garland, Charisse or Caron, Astaire would woo Hepburn, Vera-Ellen or Hayworth and be showered with not only success in love but worldly success as well. Love and success went hand-in-hand in the world of musicals. Vincente Minnelli, director of *Meet Me in St Louis* (1944), *The Pirate*

(1948), *An American in Paris* (1951) and *The Band Wagon* (1953), raised the musical genre to new heights, as did Gene Kelly and Stanley Donan when they directed *On the Town* (1949), *Singin' in the Rain* (1952) and *It's Always Fair Weather* (1955).

Musicals were among the first genres to be discarded with the break-up of the studio system in the 1950s. They were expensive to make, required a large body of permanent employees to produce, and were deemed commercially risky if written especially for the screen. When MGM divested itself of stars such as Kelly, Garland and Astaire, then the writing was on the wall. From the mid-50s on, the only musicals made, by and large, were film versions of Broadway hits. Since the heyday of musicals, there have been talented individuals such as Bob Fosse (*Cabaret*) and Barbra Streisand (*Funny Girl*) working in the genre, but there has been no group of people to match the

greats of the MGM musical years. The dancing MGM musical vanished with the demise of the studio as a major movie-producing factory. However, in the last few decades the musical has partly reinvented itself in movies such as *Saturday Night Fever*, *Pennies from Heaven*, *Flashdance*, *Dirty Dancing*, *A Chorus Line*, *Moulin Rouge* and *Chicago*. *Moulin Rouge* (2001) was a radical reworking of the movie musical: its stars were not singing and dancing specialists; there was practically no original music written for the movie; and the superfast editing techniques did not allow the audience to dwell on any shortcomings of performance. Yet somehow, it worked. *Chicago* (2002) capitalized on this new interest in musicals, winning a Best Picture Oscar.

BELOW *Bob Fosse directed* Cabaret *(1972), starring Liza Minnelli and Michael York. Fosse brought a fresh style to the movie musical, but he never really repeated the success he had with this movie.*

GANGSTER MOVIES

Between 1930 and 1932 Hollywood produced a number of gangster movies that were genuinely more radical in spirit than those of other genres. The three best known are *Little Caesar* (1931), *The Public Enemy* (1931) and *Scarface* (1932). They are morality tales, a kind of Horatio Alger success story but turned upside down and viewed from the point of view of the dispossessed of society, who have to steal and murder their way to the top because all other "normal" avenues are cut off for them. The authorities were disturbed by the social undertones of these films and forced the studios to attach moral homilies to the movies: *Little Caesar* ends with titling on the screen saying, "Rico's career had been a skyrocket, starting in the gutter and ending there." Soon, the Hays Office, set up by the movie moguls themselves to stave off external censorship and to answer increasing

protests about the moral depravity of movies, was clamping down on the manner in which gangsters were portrayed on film. Criminals were to be represented as psychopathic and isolated individuals, whom all decent citizens should despise and help the authorities to destroy.

However, the public loved the exploits of Cagney, Muni, Bogart and Raft on the screen, and all these actors became major stars, largely through their impersonations of real-life gangsters such as Al Capone and John Dillinger. The gangster genre has never been as popular again as it was in the 1930s, but since then it has produced some of Hollywood's best movies, including *The Asphalt Jungle* (1950), in which a character states that "Crime is merely a left-handed form of human endeavour", *Bonnie and Clyde* (1967), a glamorizing and myth-making treatment of the story of

ABOVE *Warren Oates played famous gangster John Dillinger in the 1973 movie* Dillinger, *which was directed by John Milius.*

1930s gangsters, and *The Godfather* and *The Godfather Part II* (1972 and 1974). All four of these films seem to imply that society is hypocritical in its attitude to crime and that the boundaries between "respectable" business, the forces of law and order, and organized and "disorganized" crime are very thin indeed. In the 1980s, movies such as *Scarface* (1983), starring Al Pacino, and *Once Upon a Time in America* (1984), directed by Sergio Leone, reflected the continuing fascination with gangsterdom and what criminals tell us about the society in which we live.

Martin Scorsese's reworking of the gangster genre in movies such as *GoodFellas* (1990), *Casino* (1995) and *Gangs of New York* (2002) have been

LEFT *James Cagney in a familiar pose as the gangster as hero. Have Hollywood movies glamorized the gangster figure?*

welcomed by audiences, whilst Warren Beatty's *Bugsy* (1991) was more in the traditional mould of the genre. These are very violent films and portray criminals as ruthless homicidal individuals who will stop at almost nothing to make their way in the world. Scorsese's gangster movies in particular push the representation of sadistic violence to uncomfortable extremes. It is reasonable to question whether this is acceptable in terms of showing it how it is or whether the audience is being invited to enjoy the violence on a prurient level. The same issues arise when the movies directed by Quentin Tarantino are discussed: *Reservoir Dogs* (1992) and *Pulp Fiction* (1994) seem to invite audiences to enjoy scenes of sadistic torture. British gangster films never had the resonance of their Hollywood

counterparts, although some British attempts at the genre have shown a tougher approach: *Get Carter, Villain, The Krays* and *The Long Good Friday.* Cockney gangsters have recently

been given a new lease of life, for example in *Lock, Stock and Two Smoking Barrels* and *Snatch.* The French have always found Hollywood gangsters irresistible, and movies such as *Rififi, Le Samouraï* and *La Balance* show their debt to the Hollywood originals. Jean-Pierre Melville's gangster movies, such as *Le Doulos* and *Le Deuxième Souffle,* pay homage to the Hollywood prototype and have more to do with style than reality. His romanticized representations of honourable criminals appeal to us, but don't expect to meet anyone like that in the real criminal world.

ABOVE *Warren Beatty turned to the gangster genre again with* Bugsy, *which was about real-life gangster Bugsy Siegel, one of the criminal fraternity who brought us the doubtful bonus of Las Vegas.*

ACTION/ADVENTURE MOVIES

Adventure movies, or "action films", exist in various guises but inevitably involve a resourceful hero, and occasionally a heroine, who come up against incredible odds and win through in the last reel. Under "adventure" we could classify the wild fantasies of the James Bond movies, the swashbucklers, historical extravaganzas, "jungle" and "desert"

ABOVE *Burt Lancaster made several swashbucklers early in his career, including* The Flame and the Arrow *(1950), directed by Jacques Tourneur.*

epics, and a whole range of "actioners" including disaster movies. Universal, when it was still a minnow studio in the 1940s and 50s, produced a series of adventures supposedly set in exotic desert locations but actually shot in local sandpits; these movies were irreverently known as "tits and sand" in the trade, because of the opportunity they gave the studio to put its glamorous stars in skimpy costumes and to shoot cheaply on the back lot.

Just as weepies were intended to appeal predominantly to a female audience, so action films were perceived as appealing to men, hence the creation of major male stars who stood for adventure in the public mind: Douglas Fairbanks Senior and Junior, Clark Gable, Errol Flynn, Tyrone Power, Gary Cooper, Stewart Granger, Charlton Heston, Alan Ladd, Sabu, Cornel Wilde, John Payne, Sean Connery, John Wayne and Harrison Ford. Women inevitably played second fiddle to the male stars in these movies, but female names such as Yvonne De Carlo, Rhonda Fleming, Paulette Goddard, Susan Hayward, Dorothy Lamour, Maureen O'Sullivan and Maria Montez would appear above the title in many a routine actioner.

If particular stars were associated with action movies, so were individual directors who acquired a reputation for being able to keep the action moving while providing enough thrills and spills to please audiences. Among these were Irwin Allen (*The Lost World, The Poseidon Adventure, The Towering Inferno*), Cecil B. De Mille (*Reap the Wild Wind, Unconquered, Northwest Mounted Police*), Henry Hathaway (*Lives of a Bengal Lancer, Prince Valiant, North to Alaska*), Howard Hawks (*Only Angels Have Wings, Hatari, The Big Sky*), John Huston (*Moby Dick, The Treasure of the Sierra Madre,*

RIGHT Bullitt *is one of the best cop action movies ever made, with a stunning car chase up and down the hills of San Francisco at the heart of it.*

The African Queen), Zoltan Korda (*Sanders of the River, Elephant Boy, The Four Feathers, The Thief of Bagdad*) and Raoul Walsh (*They Drive by Night, They Died with their Boots On, Gentleman Jim, Captain Horatio Hornblower*). Sub-genres under the umbrella of action films would also include boxing movies, motor-racing films and movies adapted from novels by John Buchan and Rider Haggard.

The Hollywood actioner could always be relied upon to throw up some absurd casting, for example Alan Ladd as a knight of the Round Table (*The Black Knight*) or Tony Curtis as an Arab in a tale of Arabian adventure (*Son of Ali Baba*) or as a Viking (*The Vikings*). Saturday morning serials were basically actioners stretched thinly over countless episodes (*The Perils of Pauline, Flash Gordon, Captain Marvel* and *Batman*). Each episode would leave the hero or heroine in

MICHAEL DOUGLAS · KATHLEEN TURNER · DANNY DeVITO

LE DIAMANT DU NIL

THE JEWEL OF THE NILE

ABOVE *The 1985 sequel to* Romancing the Stone, The Jewel of the Nile *scarcely takes itself seriously in the vein of modern adventure movies.*

some dreadful predicament from which no apparent escape was possible. The Indiana Jones series was Spielberg's affectionate tribute to the good old days of Saturday morning cinema when you cheered the goodies and hissed the baddies. The *Mission Impossible* movies took their inspiration, if that is the word, from a 1960s television show, whilst the *Jurassic Park* movies harked back to movies such as *King Kong* and *The*

Lost World. Comic-book heroes such as Batman, Dick Tracy, Superman and Spiderman have found their adventures transferred to the big screen as what was once despised as low culture has become respectable. These comic-book hero movies mostly have a knowing, self-conscious, parodying tone to them, as though the film-makers are saying to

LEFT *John Woo graduated from making action movies in Hong Hong to big-budget Hollywood movies such as* Mission Impossible II *(2000), which again starred Tom Cruise as the good guy, Ethan Hunt.*

ABOVE *The dinosaurs in* Jurassic Park *were computer-generated, but they still scared the hell out of movie-goers.*

the audience, yes, we know this is ridiculous, but just share the joke with us. The *Men in Black* movies took this self-mocking tone that much further and the result was almost a total parody of the genre. *Spider-Man* (2001) was treated more respectfully, but intrinsic to these movies is an inevitable element of sending-up. We cannot take our heroes totally seriously in a real world that consistently exposes them as fraudulent.

COMEDIES

Abbott and Costello, Laurel and Hardy, the great comedians of the silents, Martin and Lewis, The Three Stooges, Fernandel, Bob Hope, Sid Field, the *Carry On* series, the *Doctor* series, the *Pink Panther* series, screwball comedy, Red Skelton, Hepburn and Tracy comedies, Preston Sturges, Ealing comedies, Mel Brooks, Woody Allen, W.C. Fields, Danny Kaye, Ernst Lubitsch, the Marx Brothers, Neil Simon, Frank Tashlin, Billy Wilder, Gene Wilder, the Farrelly brothers, Jim Carrey, Mike Myers: all these and many, many more make up some kind of Hall of Fame for cinematic comedy.

ABOVE *Groucho Marx, the only really funny Marx brother, is the one in the middle. Harpo is on the left and Chico, decidedly unfunny, is on the right.*

Comedy divides opinion like no other type of movie. Woody Allen is the funniest man alive for some people; others find that his angst-ridden attempts to provoke laughter leave them entirely unmoved. Many people still laugh at Abbott and Costello when their movies are shown on television, while many other people wonder what anyone could have ever seen in the little fat guy and his straight-man partner, although at their peak in the 1940s they were No. 1 box-office stars in America.

The fact is that nothing dates as fast as comedy, and often what people cling to when watching old comedies again is the memory of their youth and what made them laugh in the good old days. Try telling a

LEFT *Bud Abbott (the thin one) and Lou Costello (the fat one) were the top box-office comedy team in the 1940s. They still have their fervent fans today.*

contemporary young person why you think Danny Kaye movies are funny and watch the incredulous look appear on their face. And how to explain the awful fascination that *Three Stooges* movies can have with their nose-twisting, ear-pulling, thumb-wrenching sadism? Did we really find that funny in those days? Was Jerry Lewis always as inane? Did anyone, anywhere, ever find Red Skelton funny? Yes, obviously they did, because Skelton was big at the box office for a time in the 1940s. There's no accounting for taste in comedy.

For example, I have tried to appreciate the comic genius that Preston Sturges is supposed to have poured into comedies such as *The Great McGinty*, *Sullivan's Travels* and

ABOVE *Marilyn Monroe, Jack Lemmon and Tony Curtis starred in many people's favourite comedy, Some Like it Hot.*

ABOVE *Mel Brooks had a huge hit with the western spoof* Blazing Saddles *in 1974. Despite recent flops, he has retained his place at the top of the screen-comedy tree.*

Hail the Conquering Hero, but, for the life of me, I just can't see it. The *Carry On* series leaves me absolutely cold and leaves, I suspect, the rest of the world outside Britain the same way, but every time those comic epics crop up on television they get decent audiences, so somebody out there must like them. My own favourite type of Hollywood comedy, the screwball variety, is a taste that many people do not share. But for me, movies such as *Bringing Up Baby*,

ABOVE **Carry on Cleo** (1965) *was meant as a spoof of the infamous Liz Taylor movie of* Cleopatra, *which almost bankrupted 20th Century Fox. Here, Sid James as the unlikeliest Roman is seen with a very unlikely Cleopatra, Amanda Barrie.*

His Girl Friday, Ball of Fire, I Was a Male War Bride, Monkey Business, Twentieth Century, Love Crazy and numerous others had an anarchic tone and a paciness to them that made them the most enduring of screen comedies. I admire some Ealing comedies such as *The Ladykillers* and *The Man in the White Suit*, but generally find the view of British life represented in the majority of these films too cosy and self-congratulatory. Many, many would disagree.

Since the 1990s Hollywood has moved the boundaries of what was once thought to be acceptable in comedy. Now we have the gross-out comedy served up in "masterpieces" such as *There's Something About Mary, Dumb and Dumber*, the *Ace Ventura* movies, the *Police Academy* and *American Pie* series, where the main focus is on bodily functions and the grosser aspects of teenage sex. The object seems to be to make the audience groan with disgust, and this alone is deemed to be intrinsically comedic.

Only a small proportion of films survive the passing of years to impress future generations with the same impact as when they were first released. But for comedies, the job is even harder. In 2020, will Peter Sellers as Inspector Clouseau seem funny to people for whom Sellers is just a vague

ABOVE *The Monty Python team graduated from television to the big screen and had a success in 1983 with* The Meaning of Life. *Here Eric Idle, Michael Palin, Graham Chapman and Terry Jones play overgrown schoolboys, while John Cleese provides discipline.*

name from the past? Is Woody Allen's appeal a particularly contemporary one, relevant only to the 1980s and 90s? Will anyone still be watching *Three Stooges* movies in 2020? Perhaps we should leave these questions to the academics and just enjoy what we enjoy when we enjoy it.

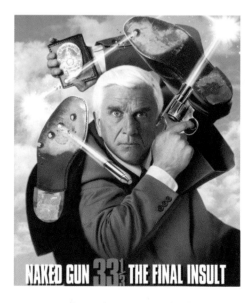

NAKED GUN 33⅓ THE FINAL INSULT

ABOVE *Leslie Nielsen resurrected a flagging screen career when he started to appear in the* Naked Gun *series of movies as Frank Drebin, the dumbest cop of them all.*

119

ROMANTIC COMEDIES

Romantic comedy is a sub-genre of comedy, and in the heyday of Hollywood was staple fare in the movie houses of the world. In the 1930s stars such as Joan Crawford, Margaret Sullavan, Katharine

ABOVE *An early example of romantic comedy. Laurence Olivier (before he became a "serious" actor) and Merle Oberon starred in the British movie* The Divorce of Lady X *(1938).*

Hepburn, Myrna Loy, Claudette Colbert, Cary Grant, Clark Gable and William Powell were regularly cast in romantic comedies, which were big at the box office. Consider these 1930s movies: *It Happened One Night, The Shop Around the Corner, Quality Street, Alice Adams, Sylvia Scarlett, The Divorce of Lady X, Shopworn Angel, Dancing Lady, Wife versus Secretary* and *Bringing Up Baby* (a screwball romantic comedy). The plot consisted of variations on

hero and heroine "meeting cute" (for example, they bump into each other or get tangled in each other's clothes), falling in love, having a misunderstanding often involving one or more potential love rivals, then further complications of plot until they reach the resolution with the promise of marriage and happiness-ever-after. The goal of all romantic comedy of that time was the marriage of the hero and heroine.

By the 1940s and 50s, the sex war had sharpened and exchanges between the sexes on screen became slightly franker and more edgy. The Spencer Tracy–Katharine Hepburn comedies – *Woman of the Year, Adam's Rib, Pat and Mike* and *The Desk Set* – represented the relationship of the sexes in a transitional stage in which women were breaking free from more traditional roles and the men were resisting these changes. Judy Holliday made romantic comedies in which even her dumb-blonde persona was seen to be making progress

RIGHT *Woody Allen adopted the persona of Humphrey Bogart to help him in his wooing of Diane Keaton in the 1972* Play It Again, Sam.

ABOVE *Ross Hunter produced a series of Rock Hudson–Doris Day romantic comedies which proved very popular. In the 1959* Pillow Talk *Rock Hudson, as per usual, pursued the virtue of reluctant Doris Day.*

against male intransigence: *Born Yesterday, The Marrying Kind, It Should Happen to You, Phffft!* and *The Solid Gold Cadillac* are examples. Whatever good fortune befell the heroine, however, her ultimate wish was represented as being married to a good man and having a family.

This, indeed, was the raison d'être of the women played by Doris Day in a series of mainly Ross Hunter-produced comedies in the late 1950s and 60s. Her character's main object was to resist the lascivious advances of a male lothario and attain a state of marriage without losing her virginity. Day's virtue was threatened by various male stars such as Clark Gable, Rock Hudson, Cary Grant and Rod Taylor in movies such as *Teacher's Pet, Pillow Talk, Lover Come Back, Move Over Darling, That Touch of Mink* and *Send Me No Flowers.*

Just as the Audrey Hepburn-starring *Roman Holiday* had been the romantic comedy of the 1950s (Hepburn played a Princess Margaret-type character on the loose in Rome), so *Breakfast at Tiffany's* with Hepburn paired with George Peppard became the most famous of Hollywood romantic comedies in the 1960s. Hepburn also starred with Albert Finney in *Two for the Road*, directed by Stanley Donen.

If the lovers in these romantic comedies never made it to bed, that is not the case with recent examples of the sub-genre: the problem is not whether the hero and heroine have sex together, but whether their relationship will survive beyond that. Doris Day's resolute defence of her virginity has long since been forgotten; now in the movies it is just as likely that the heroine will make

BELOW *Hugh Grant and Andie MacDowell meet for the first time in the hugely successful British romantic comedy* Four Weddings and a Funeral *(1994).*

the first moves and it is the hero who feels his freedom under threat. Romantic comedy can still be very big at the box office indeed, as *When Harry Met Sally..., Four Weddings and a Funeral, Notting Hill, As Good As It Gets, Sliding Doors, You've Got Mail* and *Bridget Jones's Diary* have shown. The stars of romantic comedy now are Tom Hanks, Meg Ryan, Gwyneth Paltrow, Hugh Grant, Julia Roberts,

ABOVE *Meg Ryan and Billy Crystal discuss the nature of relationships between men and women in the hit romantic comedy* When Harry Met Sally... *(1989).*

Helen Hunt, Renée Zellweger and Reese Witherspoon. Romantic comedy has caught up with the mores of the times, but essentially it exploits the same subject matter it has always done: love between two people.

121

EPICS

The cinema has always tried to provide spectacle for mass audiences. After all, the camera can go anywhere and record scenes of enormous vistas and in great detail. Through the skills of their set and costume designers, the technological and material resources of cinema can recreate any period of history, any imaginary world, any vision of writers and directors. Nowadays, "epic" backgrounds such as vast amphitheatres filled with bloodthirsty crowds can be generated through computer technology. Think of the savings the producers can make from not employing all those thousands of extras! Ever since they became a mass entertainment, movies have tried

ABOVE *The 1956 version of* The Ten Commandments *was director Cecil B. De Mille's second attempt to film this biblical story. Charlton Heston was Moses and Yul Brynner was The Pharaoh. It was a toss-up who was the more wooden.*

to provide spectacles that no other art or entertainment medium can rival in their size, authenticity and sheer opulence.

The Birth of a Nation was the cinema's first great spectacle and from then on many producers and directors have attempted to impress us with the grandness of their designs, the extravagance of their concepts, their devotion to reproducing a historical period and to rewriting history itself.

Unfortunately, along the way, authenticity was often the first casualty, so we saw such errors of taste as John Wayne as a Roman centurion at the foot of the Cross mouthing, "Truly, this was the son of Gawd." Tony Curtis, complete with Brooklyn accent, would play Roman slaves, and Victor Mature would

ABOVE *Victor Mature pulls down the temple in the 1949 epic* Samson and Delilah, *which also starred Hedy Lamarr.*

wrestle with stuffed lions. Epics would become the excuse for excessive religiosity in Cecil B. De Mille's spectacles or for viewing female stars in skimpy costumes as with Lana Turner in *The Prodigal.* Somehow scripts tended to be more leaden for epics – as Howard Hawks said about the dreadful *Land of the Pharaohs,* which

ABOVE *Tolstoy's* War and Peace *received the Hollywood epic treatment in 1956. It starred Audrey Hepburn, a miscast Henry Fonda and Mel Ferrer.*

122

ABOVE Spartacus (1960) was one of the few literate Hollywood epics. It managed to be about something other than violent action set against a Roman background.

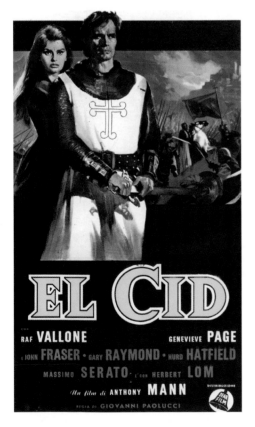

ABOVE El Cid (1961), directed by Anthony Mann, starred Charlton Heston and had a fine musical score by Miklós Rózsa.

he directed, "I never knew how a Pharaoh talked." How does Moses talk; how does a Roman slave leading a rebellion against the Roman Empire talk? Indeed, does Ben-Hur need to talk at all? There have been few literate epics but, then, the mass movie audience don't want Shakespeare when they pay their money to see an epic. They want size, action, spectacle, thrills, good triumphing over evil, and romance.

Only a handful of epics stand up to any test of real quality; the vast majority are best enjoyed as cinema at its most ostentatious and its most vulgar. You do not go to an epic to be educated about a historical period or learn how people lived in past times. You go to an epic to be impressed by the size of things and to wonder at the effort that went into the enterprise.

We usually think of epics as taking place in the distant past, produced by De Mille and starring the inevitable Charlton Heston, but movies such as *Titanic* are epics in a light disguise: the object is to serve up great spectacle, currently with the lavish use of special computer-generated effects. This was also true of *Gladiator*, which is in the tradition of *Spartacus* and *The Last Days of Pompeii*. *The Lord of the Rings* series, adapted from J.R.R. Tolkien's books, are epic in scale and embrace legend, myths and spirituality while telling a simple tale of the struggle of good and evil. Indeed, not many epics have room to allow for shades of grey: delineation of character and motive is not a top priority in this genre.

With the success of *Gladiator* and *Titanic*, other epics will follow fast on their heels. However, those overtly religious epics such as *The Ten Commandments* and *The Greatest Story*

ABOVE Boris Pasternak's novel Doctor Zhivago was given epic screen treatment in the 1965 MGM movie directed by David Lean and starred Julie Christie, Omar Sharif and Rod Steiger.

Ever Told (1965) are unlikely to make a reappearance, unless the religious right's influence in Hollywood and America in general takes a grip. It is a fact that epics are conservative in the political and social attitudes they embrace: *Spartacus* was one of the few liberal epics ever made. Generally epics take the side of nice kings and queens as opposed to nasty rebels.

ABOVE Gladiator (2000) was the first Roman epic Hollywood made for many years. It proved that this kind of epic still had legs at the box office.

FILM NOIR

Strictly speaking, *film noir* is not a genre. It is a body of films that emerged from Hollywood between 1941 and 1958 that shared stylistic and thematic concerns. The term was first used by French critics when they noticed the "blackness" of look and theme common to the American movies released in France after the Liberation. Perhaps because they had

ABOVE *Gene Tierney played a neurotic woman under the control of an evil psychiatrist, Jose Ferrer, in the 1950* Whirlpool.

their determinedly shadowy images and nihilistic view of human nature. However, an opposing view of Hollywood *film noir* points to the war-time and immediate post-war restrictions placed on American film-makers by the US government. Hollywood had to cut down on its use of lighting and sets because resources were needed for the war effort. Thus, the shadowy, dark look of wartime movies came not from the film-makers' gloomy view of the world, but from technological necessity: they could not use extensive lighting, so they used dark sets lit by a few lights or filmed at night. One additional effect of the muted lighting was that it

disguised the reuse of old sets again and again because of the restrictions on set-building.

Whatever the origins of *film noir*, certain thematic concerns and familiar plot lines are apparent in the body of

ABOVE *Tyrone Power had one of his best screen roles in* Nightmare Alley *(1947)*.

been cut off for four years from American films, the critics remarked on how different these movies were from the standard pre-war Hollywood product with its glossy, high-key lighting and upbeat, reassuring message. These *films noirs* were bleak social documents, turning a disenchanted eye on the contemporary American scene and uncovering a society full of anxieties and divisions.

The film-makers who made the *films noirs* were perhaps influenced by German Expressionism and Italian Neo-realism. Expatriate European directors such as Wilder, Preminger, Ophuls, Siodmak and Curtiz made some of the best-known *noirs* with

ABOVE *Humphrey Bogart and Lauren Bacall try to work out the plot in the 1947 thriller* The Big Sleep. *The stars married in real life but Bogart died prematurely in 1957.*

Falcon, Double Indemnity, The Big Sleep, Out of the Past, Crossfire and Touch of Evil.

If you are being pedantic, the term *film noir* can only really be applied to those black-and-white movies that were made between, say, 1941 (*The Maltese Falcon*) and 1958 (*Touch of Evil*). However, *film noir* remains an influence on movie-makers around the world. In recent years, two movie hits have self-consciously paid homage to *film noir*: *The Usual Suspects* and *L.A. Confidential*.

BELOW Touch of Evil (1958), *directed by Orson Welles, is often identified as the last movie made that truly belonged to the authentic film noir tradition.*

ABOVE The Third Man (1949) *was a brilliant British* film noir *directed by Carol Reed, and starring Orson Welles.*

films dubbed *noir*. Very often a *film noir* is about a male protagonist encountering a femme fatale, for example, who uses her sexual attractiveness to manipulate him into murder. She then double-crosses the sap until order is restored by the destruction of this powerful female figure, often at the cost of the hero's life. Perhaps *film noir* is misogynist in its general representation of women: the women are beautiful but duplicitous, predatory and promiscuous. This trend in wartime and post-war American movies may have had something to do with the uncertain relationship between the sexes due to wartime dislocations and suspicions about what had gone on while the boys were away at war. In addition, millions of women had their first opportunity to work during the war years, and this fed male paranoia that women were breaking out and refusing to play their "correct" roles in society as mothers and wives. This anxiety was fed into the movies that Hollywood made in order to "cheer" wartime audiences.

a film by
Orson
Welles

with Orson Welles + Charlton Heston
Janet Leigh + Marlene Dietrich

Film noir was often the product of the "B" picture system, whereby the studios produced low-budget films to fill the lower half of double bills. As a result these "B" pictures were not given the same scrutiny as the "A" pictures, which allowed creative directors and writers the freedom to experiment and handle themes that would have been out of bounds on more expensive products. The result was masterpieces such as *The Maltese*

RIGHT A late film noir is Roman Polanski's Chinatown (1974), *a deliberate homage to the tradition of the genre.*

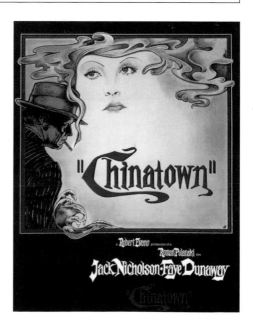

Robert Evans
Roman Polanski
Jack Nicholson·Faye Dunaway
Chinatown

HORROR MOVIES

Audiences love to be scared, and film-makers have learned to serve up ready-made nightmares on demand. Horror films came out of the tradition of European Gothic novels by way of Mary Godwin and Bram Stoker. Cinema, of all the art forms, is nearest to the dream state: we sit in the dark watching huge figures on a screen enact our fantasies and fears. Horror films deal with our nightmares, the fears of mankind, the horror of the irrational and the unknown, and the horror of man himself. They embrace the classic demonic myths of Frankenstein and Dracula, the concept of nature that turns abnormal, and the horror of human personality. Horror is the

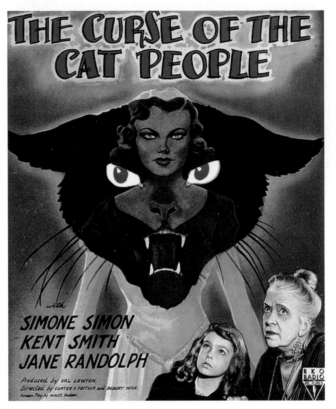

ABOVE *Tod Browning directed the strange* Freaks (1932) and The Devil-Doll (1936). *There is still a certain fascination about these movies, as this re-release of a Browning double bill reflects.*

creature, the blood-sucking vampire, the fiendish scientist, the ghoul, or Freddy with the murderous, nightmarish nails. Horror is all around us in the everyday world: it is a shadow on the walls of a deserted swimming-pool (*Cat People*), it is a hesitant, shy and psychopathic young man in a motel (*Psycho*), or it is a man with "love" and "hate" tattooed on his hands (*The Night of the Hunter*).

Some observers see the horror film as an expression of our subconscious wish to smash the norms that oppress us. For example, many horror films are located within the family situation. In horror films the underside of normality is exposed and the irrational chaos beneath respectability and convention explodes and threatens to engulf society. As in all genres, however, the monstrous has to be defeated and the norms restored. We are able to indulge our rebellious instincts for a while before the status quo wins through. While watching the horror movie, we half-long for the

LEFT *Val Lewton was one of the best-known horror movie producers. The Curse of the Cat People was the 1944 sequel to the highly successful but subtly scary* Cat People (1942).

forces of chaos to win, but fear at the same time what that chaos will reveal about ourselves.

In the 1950s the British company Hammer Films began to rework the myths of Dracula, Frankenstein, werewolves, vampires and all the other elements of the classic horror movie. Their models were clearly the Universal Studios' horror movies of the 1930s, but Hammer mostly shot in colour and with reasonable budgets for sets and costumes. The result is

ABOVE *In the 1950s and 60s the British company Hammer Films reworked some of the old Universal horror movies. Here is one their more successful efforts,* Horror of Dracula (aka Dracula, 1958).

126

ABOVE *The other face of horror: a Hammer zombie relaxes and smiles for the camera in his lunch hour during the shooting of* The Mummy's Shroud *(1967).*

BELOW *Joan Crawford carved out for herself a mini-career late in her life as the heroine, or otherwise, of horror movies such as* I Saw What You Did, *directed by horror specialist William Castle in 1965.*

that the early Hammer productions look fairly sumptuous, so whatever tosh the story serves up, the movies at least look good. Two major horror stars emerged from this cycle of Hammer movies: Peter Cushing (much the better actor of the two) and Christopher Lee. Cushing's first effort in the horror stakes was *The Curse of Frankenstein* (1957), then came *Horror of Dracula* (1958), *The Revenge of Frankenstein* (1958) and *The Hound of the Baskervilles* (1959). Cushing became a star of horror movies and he went to make many other Hammer films, as well as working for other producers of the genre. Lee took the title role in *Horror of Dracula* (he and Cushing were very often paired in these movies), then made *Corridors of Blood*, *The Man Who Could Cheat Death* and *The Mummy* in quick succession. He, like Cushing, acquired a wide fan base of horror addicts, and he has scarcely strayed from the genre since. He also played Dr Fu Manchu in a couple of undistinguished movies and Dracula in several sequels.

Since the early 1980s Hollywood has continued to mine the horror genre: in the *Halloween* series, the *Freddy Kruger/Nightmare on Elm Street* movies, a succession of movies adapted from Stephen King sources (*Carrie*, *Christine*, *The Shining*, *Misery*), reworkings of the ghost story (*The Sixth Sense*, *The Others*) and a knowing send-up of the genre in the *Scream* series of movies. The genre will never die out, as long as there is a

ABOVE *Christopher Lee was a star of Hammer Films. In the 1970* Scars of Dracula *he played Count Dracula yet again.*

teenage audience out there who want to be alternatively frightened and amused by the nightmares that the makers of horror movies can think up.

127

ABOVE *Donnie Darko (2002) is a half-horror, half sci-fi movie, but it deals with familiar content: the alienation of a teenager which manifests itself in horrific imaginings and dark deeds.*

SCIENCE FICTION MOVIES

Bug-eyed monsters, aliens with incredibly high IQs, invaders that act suspiciously like Cold War enemies, insubstantial jelly-like creatures that mean no harm to us earthlings, E.T., the translucent beings who emerge from the gigantic spaceship in *Close Encounters of the Third Kind*, the nasty alien out to get Mel Gibson and family in *Signs*: all of these are cinematic manifestations of our dreams about space and those unknown creatures that may or may not inhabit it.

In the 1950s, aliens – whether invading the earth or encountered when explorers ventured into space – were invariably hostile and subversive. A notable exception was Michael Rennie as Klaatu in *The Day the Earth Stood Still*: he spoke like an Englishman who had been to a public school (perhaps he had been to Eton?), was very cool and collected

ABOVE *Ed Wood's* Plan 9 from Outer Space *(1959) was so bad that it won itself a multitude of fans. It is definitely one of the worst movies ever made.*

ABOVE *Forbidden Planet (1956) is loosely based on Shakespeare's* The Tempest *and is rated as one of the better sci-fi movies of the 1950s.*

even when faced with the wickedness of earthlings, and showed extreme politeness to one and all as he tried to save us from ourselves.

However, this was the exception to the rule. Most aliens in 1950s movies were bad, and I mean really bad. This comic-book view of extra-terrestrials perhaps suited the politics of the Cold War, which was at its height then, when anybody thought to be "un-American" was suspected of Communism and subversion. The 1940s and 50s was

the era of the McCarthyite hearings in Hollywood when liberal film-makers suspected of subversion had their careers ruined by association with Communism. SF films in the 50s were employed as parables for their times: to warn against alien beings taking over the minds and territory of Americans, or as a reminder of the dangers of conformity and paranoia, as in *Invasion of the Body Snatchers* (1956). In actual fact, that movie can be interpreted in two ways: as a

ABOVE *The third of the* Planet of the Apes *series,* Escape from the Planet of the Apes *(1971), is rated as the best of the sequels in this science-fiction series.*

warning against a spreading virus of intolerance and hysteria, or about how communities can be taken over by subversives right under the noses of honest citizens.

However, by the 1970s and 80s, with the Cold War receding, aliens began to be represented as benevolent. In the 1950s the military and government agencies had been represented as saving the USA from alien invasion. Now the individual had to protect him or herself against these very agencies in order to make contact with the aliens. Consider Spielberg's movies *Close Encounters of the Third Kind* and *E.T.* In *Close Encounters* the Richard Dreyfuss character and like-minded people have to fight the oppression of the authorities in order to meet the friendly aliens. When those wobbly creatures leave the spaceship at the end of the movie, they bypass the government personnel who have been trained to go into space with them, instead heading for the ordinary joes and jills who have only

good will in their hearts and a desire to leave everything behind them for a jaunt into another galaxy. Similarly, in the same director's *E.T.*, it is not the sinister government technicians and scientists who save the cuddly extra-terrestrial and treat him like a human being (well, not exactly, but you get the idea), but the empathizing youngsters who learn how to fly their bicycles in the process of saving him.

However, old attitudes die hard, and *Independence Day* (1996), *Mars Attacks!* (1996) and *Signs* (2002) have resurrected the evil alien figure to

ABOVE *E.T. (1982) was one of the most successful sci-fi movies ever made, and it represented aliens as well-disposed beings.*

trouble our daydreams. But now that old enemies have become new friends and the Cold War is officially dead, how will future cinematic aliens be represented, and who will they stand for in our dreams about the vast, unknowable reaches of space?

129

ABOVE *The* Star Wars *series went back in time for the beginning of the saga in a galaxy far, far away with* Episode 1: The Phantom Menace *(1999).*

LOVE STORIES

By "love stories" or "romantic movies", one usually means movies in which the main interest is in the romantic involvement of the two leads. Some people, on that basis, would argue that *Gone with the Wind* is a love story about Scarlett O'Hara and Rhett Butler rather than a civil-war epic. Similarly, *Casablanca* is about the tragic love between Bogart and

ABOVE *The Seventh Veil (1945) may be a perverse love story, but a love story it is under all the psychological melodrama. In the final reel Ann Todd, a disturbed pianist, realizes she has been in love with her guardian, the sadistic James Mason, all the while.*

Bergman rather than a thriller involving the Nazis, Claude Rains as a Vichy policeman and the Resistance. Some love stories are located in specific periods and are enacted amidst important events, such as *The Way We Were*, which deals with the McCarthyite period in Hollywood

but is more about the on-off romance between Streisand and Redford's characters. Who remembers very much about the Spanish Civil War from *For Whom the Bell Tolls?* But everyone remembers the Gary Cooper–Ingrid Bergman love affair.

Romantic love is a staple element in almost all Hollywood movies, even in genres such as horror, sci-fi, war or western movies. The producer would always say, "Where's the love interest?" The idea was that if there was a love story between the hero and heroine, then the appeal of a genre movie could be widened and, specifically, a female audience could be wooed into the cinema. I wish I could say things have got more sophisticated since the 1990s, but there is little evidence of that. Love interest is still pretty high on any self-respecting producer's list, even when the story and subject matter do not naturally call for it.

The British have made their share of romantic movies, but until the 1960s they were usually of the tight-lipped, blouse-buttoned variety – such as the most famous of them, *Brief Encounter*, where Celia Johnson is appalled when Trevor Howard arranges for them to borrow a friend's flat for some adulterous love-making. Oh,

LEFT *The most famous love story of the British cinema is Brief Encounter (1946), directed by David Lean from a script by Noel Coward. It starred Celia Johnson and Trevor Howard as very genteel, illicit lovers.*

the shame of it all! Indeed, lovers had to be very discreet in the movies right until the early 60s when the Production Code that ruled what you could and could not show in movies began to break down. British movies such as *Room at the Top*, *The Girl with Green Eyes* and all those films about Swinging London swept most of the restrictions aside. But romance was not about sex and bedroom scenes: it was about Katharine Hepburn being swept off her feet by Rossano Brazzi in *Summer Madness*; it was about Montgomery Clift and Elizabeth Taylor in *A Place in the Sun*; it was Jennifer Jones waiting on a windy hill for the return of William Holden in *Love is a Many Splendored Thing*; it was Joan Fontaine in *Rebecca* and *Letter from an Unknown Woman*, expiring of love for Laurence Olivier and Louis Jourdan.

ABOVE *The 1973* The Way We Were *was one of the most successful love stories of the 1970s. Starring Barbra Streisand and Robert Redford, it was partly set against Hollywood in the 1940s.*

130

For a while now, there have been few movies that are straight romances. There has been lots of explicit sex in movies, but straightforward romance has seemed to decline. There have been a few movies that portray gay or lesbian love affairs, but they have generally failed to attract a wider audience. Perhaps the relationships between men and women were too fraught during the period that saw a battle for equal rights by women for conventional romantic movies to be that popular. There has been a

BELOW Manhattan, *along with* Annie Hall, *may ultimately be seen as Woody Allen's major achievements in the cinema. With a wonderful score of George Gershwin tunes,* Manhattan *is not only about the love stories of the characters, but a hymn of love to the city itself.*

continuing obsession with sex in the movies, but even sex is shown to be a dangerous and potentially destructive instinct when indulged (*Fatal Attraction, Jagged Edge, The Morning After*). One 1980s love story, *Falling in Love* with Robert De Niro and Meryl Streep as the lovers, failed disastrously at the box office. In many ways, this movie was a throwback to the days of the great movie love story with two of the biggest contemporary stars playing opposite one another, but it failed to click with the general public.

However, in this post-feminist era, the time may once more be ripe for the return of the hankie-sodden

ABOVE The Age of Innocence (1993) *was adapted from Edith Wharton's novel, and starred Daniel Day-Lewis, Michelle Pfeiffer and Winona Ryder. It was an example of a subtle love story that exposed the hypocrisies of respectable society.*

love story, as the success of *Shakespeare in Love, The English Patient* and *Captain Corelli's Mandolin* show.

MELODRAMAS, WEEPIES OR WOMEN'S PICTURES

Hollywood took over melodrama from the "penny dreadfuls" and 19th-century theatre. Melodrama has always been viewed as the poor relation of tragedy and realism, but the works of important novelists such as Dickens and Dostoevsky contain plenty of melodramatic incidents and climaxes. Silent movies lent themselves to melodramatic excess; when only the image and gesture communicated meaning, then actors and directors had to hook into the melodramatic tradition to tell their stories and express feeling. Acting

ABOVE *Jane Wyman makes all the usual female sacrifices in the melodramatic weepie* The Blue Veil *(1951).*

ABOVE *The 1949* Little Women *is quintessentially a women's picture as seen through the eyes of Hollywood. The important characters are all female, it is based in the family and concerns the loves and aspirations of the female characters. Here, June Allyson gives advice to Margaret O'Brien.*

styles in the silent movie era borrowed from the tradition of acting in stage melodramas (and from mime).

Hollywood producers thought largely in stereotypes when considering audiences, so it was at the female audience that most melodramas were directed because of

the appeal that the subject matter was thought to have for women. These movies came to be known as "weepies" or "women's pictures" because of the excessive emotion they supposedly provoked in the largely female audience. However, they provided the opportunity for powerful female characters to be represented on the screen, and some independent-minded stars were created by the genre: Davis, Crawford, De Havilland and Stanwyck. These were the female stars that women were expected to identify with, the stars who acted out on screen the kind of challenges and anxieties experienced by most women – according to the ideas of Hollywood scriptwriters, at least.

The term "women's picture" can embrace several genres, from melodrama to love story to romantic comedy. However, to the traditional Hollywood producer, a women's picture meant tears shed by the

audience because of the sacrifices made by the women characters and the courage shown by these representations of womanhood in adverse circumstances – whether those were brought about by the perfidious male sex, social conditions, personal blights such as the sudden onset of illness or even lack of attractiveness, familial oppression, ungrateful children, broken or hopeless love affairs, or a combination of all of those factors. All of the afore-mentioned stars made serious sacrifices on screen for the sake of

ABOVE *Ann Sheridan was a regular in women's pictures of the 1940s. Here she is in* Nora Prentiss *(1947), playing a singer who ruins a doctor's life.*

132

ABOVE *The MGM star Greer Garson was closely identified with the women's picture genre. Here she dallies with Leo Genn in* The Miniver Story *(1950).*

There were several subgenres within the genre of melodrama: two were the maternal melodrama in which a mother figure was variously scorned, neglected or sacrificed for her children, and the family melodrama in which the institution of the family was put under strain and finally reinforced. There was also the melodrama of romantic love, in which the female protagonist was wooed, abandoned, tricked or seduced but usually ended up with the man of her choice. The ideological purpose of these movies was to reinforce female roles. But, by making women the pivotal figures in the story, they also raised questions about what women should do with their lives, and created powerful role models for millions of cinema-goers. Katharine Hepburn, Bette Davis and Barbara Stanwyck were early versions of the liberated women on our screens today.

Bette Davis and her ilk occasionally had to resort to guns and murder to get their way, but generally they never went so far as Susan Sarandon and Geena Davis in *Thelma and Louise*, who leave their partners, take to the road, shoot guns off, become the target of a police chase across the country and end up driving off a cliff to their deaths. *Thelma and Louise* was a merger

ABOVE *A classic women's picture of the 1960s is* The VIPs *(1963), which starred Elizabeth Taylor and Richard Burton. Liz is seen here with Louis Jourdan.*

of the female buddy movie with the melodramatic thriller and the road movie that showed women contemplating a future without men — indeed, what they were escaping from was men. It was hugely popular, so it must have struck a chord with a lot of people.

The traditional women's picture may have vanished, but movie producers know that it is very often the woman in a partnership who chooses which movie a couple go to see. When more than half of the cinema audience is composed of women, then whatever producers think will appeal to this female audience will determine what movies get made.

husbands, lovers, children, parents, friends or society in general. "We know", these films seemed to be saying to the female audience, "how hard your life can be and how undervalued you are, and we are bearing testimony to that!"

133

LEFT *Patricia Roc was a star of the 1940s and 50s in Britain, starring in love stories such as* Something Money Can't Buy *(1952). Here she is with co-star Anthony Steel.*

WAR MOVIES

LEFT *One of the better Hollywood war movies was the 1949 Twelve O'Clock High, which showed war as hell, avoided false heroics and represented the cost in individual terms.*

A BRIDGE TOO FAR

Joseph E. Levine presents

A BRIDGE TOO FAR

OUT OF THE SKY COMES THE SCREEN'S MOST INCREDIBLE SPECTACLE OF MEN AND WAR!

All major movie-producing nations have made war movies to attract a mass audience who either perceive them as a kind of adventure yarn or as an authentic attempt to reproduce the experience of war on the screen. War movies have been used as propaganda by all nations, especially in times of war, or in the aftermath of wars, when morale has to be kept high or national pride and mythology have to be celebrated. As a result, too many war movies in the past have been exercises in jingoism or self-congratulation; too few have represented war authentically. "War is hell!" is a plea made by intensely patriotic and anti-war movies alike. Many movies, while pointing to the horror of war, simultaneously indulge in the most dishonest heroic posturings and simplification of the issues and of who the good and bad guys are. Such films are really westerns under a different guise.

However, there have been honourable exceptions to this jingoistic rule. *All Quiet on the Western Front* (1930) and *A Walk in the Sun* (1945) were both directed by Lewis Milestone and both concentrated on the realities of war and not on false heroics. The 1949 *Twelve O'Clock High* was of the war-is-hell school, but managed to show the ravages that the strain of military life in wartime can lead to in even the strongest of men. The 1957 *Paths of Glory*, directed by Stanley Kubrick, is one of the finest

A BRIDGE TOO FAR (M)

starring (in alphabetical order)

**Dirk Bogarde
James Caan
Michael Caine
Sean Connery
Edward Fox
Elliott Gould
Gene Hackman
Anthony Hopkins
Hardy Kruger
Laurence Olivier
Ryan O'Neal
Robert Redford
Maximilian Schell
Liv Ullmann**

From the book by
Cornelius Ryan
Screenplay by
William Goldman
Produced by
Joseph E. Levine
and
Richard P. Levine
Directed by
Richard Attenborough
United Artists
A Transamerica Company

ABOVE *Richard Attenborough's 1977 movie about the debacle of the 1944 Arnhem parachute drops,* A Bridge Too Far.

and most powerful of all war movies. Strictly speaking not an anti-war movie, it still manages to indict the military mentality that can blithely send men to their certain deaths in the name of glory. Robert Aldrich's *Too Late the Hero* (1970) has a refreshingly cynical anti-war tone, which does not quite erase the memory of that other Aldrich-directed movie *The Dirty Dozen* (1967), which in the final analysis glorifies killing. Most Hollywood war movies have been too similar to the objectionable John Wayne-produced *The Green Berets* (1968), propagating a facile patriotism and mindless love of militarism.

ABOVE *John Wayne made many war movies. Here in* The Longest Day *(1962), he relaxes on the Normandy beaches before taking on the whole German army.*

ABOVE *Kenneth More starred as Douglas Bader, the flying ace who lost both his legs but who climbed back into the cockpit, in the 1956* Reach for the Sky.

If the American cinema had the mythology of the opening of the western frontier to feed off and add to, the British cinema seemed to find its central myths in World War II when Britain stood alone against the power of Germany and Japan. Post-war British cinema was obsessed with recreating the "finest hour" and reinforcing the myths surrounding "the Dunkirk spirit", the Battle of Britain, the struggle on the home front, the battle at sea and the defence of the British Empire by its loyal subjects. A large proportion of British films in the 1940s and 50s starred John Mills, Jack Hawkins, Richard Attenborough, Bryan Forbes, Peter Finch, John Gregson, Donald Sinden and Anthony Steel in a variety of uniforms showing the world and themselves how Britain did it. It was as though British film-makers were stuck in a time warp and were drawn irresistibly to the tales of POW escapes ("My turn for the tunnel, sir"), submarine warfare (Richard Attenborough turning yellow below the waves), dog-fights in the air ("I bagged a couple of gerries, Flight!") or espionage behind the enemy lines ("Your job is to convince those krauts the Normandy landings are going to take place in Spain").

This mindset changed somewhat in the 1990s with World War II epics such as *The Thin Red Line* and *Saving Private Ryan*. In *Saving Private Ryan* Steven Spielberg pulls no punches with a searing, stomach-churningly realistic depiction of the physical and mental trauma of battle. In a powerful, visceral opening sequence, the audience experiences all the tension and adrenaline rush of the US infantry as they launch into the D-Day assault on Omaha Beach. Using first-hand accounts from actual survivors, Spielberg does not flinch from showing graphic scenes of carnage and devastation, bringing home all the senselessness of war – rather than the glory. Spielberg's *Empire of the Sun* and *Schindler's List* also hammered home the idiocies and cruelty of war.

RIGHT *Oliver Stone's 1986 movie about Vietnam,* Platoon, *packs a lot of emotional power and communicates the horror of the Vietnam war almost viscerally.*

135

SOCIAL PROBLEM MOVIES

Every so often the cinema deals with a "social problem" such as racial prejudice, political unrest, alcoholism, drugs, poverty and unemployment, sexual inequality and violence towards women, or mental illness. The movies are meant to appeal to a mass audience, but because of this need to attract millions of people, the tendency has been to emphasize the personal problems of the characters at the expense of the general social issue that is ostensibly being represented. In the heyday of the studio era, Hollywood was careful not to alienate sections of public

ABOVE The Best Years of Our Lives (1946) *dealt with the problems of returning GIs after World War II. Here Dana Andrews confronts errant wife Virginia Mayo.*

opinion, and thereby endanger box-office returns; studios had to contend with multifarious pressure groups such as the Catholic Legion of Decency, the American Legion, the Daughters of the Revolution and frequently bigoted local censorship boards, all of which might put a seal of disapproval on a film – a move that could have a major impact on how well it did at the box office. The powerful Legion of

RIGHT *In the 1947 movie* The Beginning or the End, *Hollywood took on the subject of the development of the atomic bomb. Was it OK because it was in the hands of the good guys or had a genie been unleashed from the bottle that would not go back in?*

Decency's telling Catholics not to see a film because of its sexual explicitness, politics or perceived blasphemy was the stuff of producers' nightmares. Thus, many of the movies that dealt with "explosive" issues had to be so kid-gloved in their treatment that they lost credibility as serious social documents.

From the 1930s through to the 50s, the Production Code Administration, or Hays Office, which had the job of imposing censorship on all movies that aspired to being shown in American cinemas,

ABOVE *Hollywood producer and director Stanley Kramer tackled a big theme in his 1961* Judgment at Nuremberg, *which represented the trial of former Nazi leaders for war crimes. Spencer Tracy played a judge, Burt Lancaster a troubled ex-Nazi, Richard Widmark a prosecuting counsel, and Marlene Dietrich the widow of a German general.*

was a very conservative organization that saw its function as the defence of "Americanism" and the American Way of Life. Any movie that implied, for example, that racial prejudice was rife in the States would be frowned upon, so producers and writers learned to portray such manifestations as isolated examples rather than the rule. For example, in the *film noir* Crossfire, one of the themes is anti-semitism in post-war American society, but the film had to imply that the anti-semitism portrayed was merely a prejudice of one psychotic individual, played by Robert Ryan,

ABOVE The Blackboard Jungle *(1955)*
dealt with juvenile delinquency and had the
first rock 'n' roll soundtrack in any Hollywood
movie, Rock Around the Clock *played by*
Bill Haley and the Comets. Conservatives
blamed the movie for encouraging delinquency
by using such arousing music in the movie.

rather than a widespread social
phenomenon. When Ryan is shot
dead at the end of the film, the
implication is that the problem
disappears with him. Another 1940s
film, *Gentleman's Agreement,* again deals
with anti-semitism, but instead of
showing a Jewish person coming up

ABOVE *From time to time, Hollywood has*
examined the American political system.
In one of the best movies about politics,
Henry Fonda played a presidential contender
with integrity – in The Best Man *(1964),*
scripted by Gore Vidal.

against actual
prejudice, audiences
saw Gregory Peck
as a journalist
pretending to be a
Jew to find out the
extent of anti-
semitism in America.
The film manages to
be reassuring and
self-congratulatory
by individualizing
the issue and
suggesting simplistic
solutions. It is a familiar ploy.

Movies nowadays deal more
authentically and frankly with social
problems, although the tendency to
exonerate societies and institutions by
showing the occasional sinner being
punished for his transgressions is still
prevalent. In *Wall Street,* Gordon
Gekko, the character played by
Michael Douglas, is shopped by his
former disciple and the implications
are that he will go to jail for his illegal
junk bond dealing, that Wall Street is
shown to be capable of cleaning itself
up, and that all it takes is for one good
individual to stand up for morality for
things to change. Most Hollywood
films dealing with social issues are
melodramatic and fairly simplistic –
the narrative almost inevitably seeks
an ending that resolves the problem in
favour of a consensus solution.
However, Hollywood is now willing
to deal with sensitive issues such as

Aids: *Philadelphia,* for all its
sentimentality, had Tom Hanks, one
of its top male stars, playing a
homosexual dying of Aids. Think of
the possibility of James Stewart
playing such a part and you can see
how things have moved on. Yet
Hollywood will inevitably put a
coating of sugar over even the
grimmest of subjects. Even social
problem movies have to have happy
endings in Tinsel Town.

ABOVE *The dangers of the uncontrolled*
development of nuclear power stations was
explored in the 1979 The China Syndrome,
starring Jane Fonda as a concerned television
reporter, Michael Douglas as her sidekick,
and Jack Lemmon as a whistle-blowing
employee at a nuclear power station.

BELOW *Oliver Stone made* JFK *(1991)*
about a district attorney's investigation into
the Kennedy assassination. It starred Kevin
Costner as Jim Garrison, who pieces together
a conspiracy theory about the case.

137

THRILLERS

Suspense thrillers were, and are, standard products for the Hollywood studios: murder mysteries, chase thrillers, women-in-peril movies and private-eye yarns. The thriller format was often used by writers and directors to explore aspects of society and human psychology within a recognizable formula of unravelling a mystery or situating the main protagonist in danger and mayhem. Some thrillers can be classed as *film noir*, but while *film noir* crossed generic frontiers, many thrillers had no discernible *noir* elements at all.

The acknowledged master of the thriller was Alfred Hitchcock. He used the genre to manipulate his audience by means of suspense, while exploring his personal obsessions about guilt and punishment, sexuality and voyeurism, and the darker sides of human nature. For Hitchcock, plots were the means of hooking an audience. He then manipulated the members of the audience to feel as he wanted them to feel, to switch allegiances and sympathy for the characters as he wished them to do and, generally, to react on cue to the

stimuli that he controlled through the images on screen. Hitchcock seemed to be haunted by a fear of punishment and a sense of guilt – he often talked about his Catholic childhood and the fear that any authority figure, such as a priest or a policeman, would generate in him. The French critics and directors of the New Wave of the 1950s were perhaps the first to analyze seriously the thematic

ABOVE **The Man from U.N.C.L.E.** *television series was translated to the big screen in a number of films. Here Robert Vaughan and David McCallum star in* **One Spy Too Many** *(1966).*

LEFT *Hitchcock adapted* **The Birds** *(1963) from a Daphne Du Maurier story and turned it into a tense psychological drama centred on man-woman relationships and the family.*

concerns of Hitchcock the director. Francois Truffaut, for example, did a whole series of interviews with Hitchcock that were published in book form.

Does this kind of analysis treat Hitchcock with too much seriousness? After all, the man made movie thrillers, which he claimed were merely entertainments aimed at manipulating the fears and emotions of the audiences who flocked to see them. Should they not just be enjoyed for the ephemeral entertainments they

ABOVE *Director Brian De Palma has made several thrillers that pay direct homage to Hitchcock. This one,* Body Double *(1984), seemed to take its inspiration from Hitchcock's* Rear Window.

are and not over-intellectualized? This is the age-long argument about commercial movies: do critics and intellectuals make far too much of dissecting what popular movies mean to the detriment of just enjoying them? Specifically, can movie thrillers really be worth discussing in depth?

Well, does a Hitchcock movie such as *Vertigo* have deeper resonance than its labyrinthine storyline and plot twists seem to imply? I would say it has, but that any meaning it has, the

UN CERVEAU D'UN MILLIARD DE DOLLARS
"BILLION DOLLAR BRAIN"
ED BEGLEY · OSCAR HOMOLKA
and FRANÇOISE DORLEAC · PRODUCED BY HARRY SALTZMAN
DIRECTED BY KEN RUSSELL · EXECUTIVE PRODUCER ANDRE DE TOTH · NOVEL BY LEN DEIGHTON · SCREENPLAY BY JOHN McGRATH
PANAVISION COLOR by DeLuxe
EEN BREIN VAN EEN MILLIARD DOLLAR

LEFT *Michael Caine starred in the Ken Russell-directed* Billion Dollar Brain *(1967). Caine played the character of Harry Palmer, the awkward undercover agent conceived by author Len Deighton.*

viewer has to bring to it. Hitchcock weaves the tapestry; the patterns we choose to see in that tapestry are up to us. It is a similar story with Hitchcock's other masterpiece *Psycho*. On one level it is a piece of outrageous schlock, a horror movie that goes for the jugular. On another level it deals with deeper psychological issues in a highly emotional and disturbing style. The same argument can be made for a number of Hitchcock thrillers, including *Rebecca*, *Notorious*, *Strangers on a Train*, *Rear Window* and *North by Northwest*.

There have been many imitations of Hitchcock's films, notably by the American director Brian De Palma and the French director Claude Chabrol, but few have achieved the same mastery of audience manipulation that he did. Most cinema is manipulative in the sense that films seek to draw you, the viewer, into their representation of reality so that you suspend your disbelief. Thrillers depend on that suspension and on suspense as well; if you are, metaphorically, to be on the edge of your seat, you have to believe that the heroine is genuinely going to fall off the cliff or that the hero has been fatally wounded and will not recover. You have to feel the danger the protagonists are feeling, you have to want desperately for them to escape and for the villains to be defeated. To enjoy a thriller fully, your fears have to be engaged, you have to care, you have to go through agonies and suspense before relief is granted. If you are detached from the action on the screen, you might be able to admire clinically how the formula is constructed, but you are unlikely to gain much more from the experience.

BELOW LEFT AND BELOW *The* Thomas Crown Affair *has been made twice: in 1967 with Steve McQueen and Faye Dunaway, and in 1999 with Pierce Brosnan and Rene Russo. The two characters play a cat-and-mouse game as each tries to keep one step ahead of the other.*

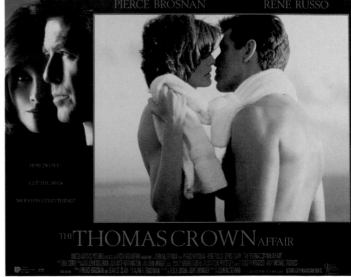

COMPUTER-GENERATED FILMS

from the creators of "toy story"

Walt Disney Pictures
Presents
A PIXAR Film
a bug's life

LEFT A Bug's Life (1998) is a computer-animated feature produced by Pixar, the same company that produced the Toy Story movies.

Special effects have become ever more sophisticated since the early days of cinema. Nowadays, film-makers dispense with models, sets, automation, blue screens and such like crude tricks. The computer rules in the movies, just as it does in many other walks of life. Computer-generated effects are here to stay – or at least until they are themselves displaced by some advanced technology that hasn't even been thought of yet.

The new whizz-kids of special effects are the children of the computer age. They work for George Lucas's Industrial Light and Magic in California or for the Disney studios, where old-fashioned animation is still alive and kicking in movies such as *Beauty and the Beast* and *The Lion King*, although animated films have become ever more complex and spectacular in the images and sounds they create.

We have to get our heads around the idea that much of what we see on screen nowadays is not real in the physical sense – the "realities" we see exist only because a computer has generated them. For example, the scenes in *Gladiator* in the Roman arena

were largely computer-generated. Only a partial set was built and a relatively small crowd used to people it; there was no amphitheatre as in, say, *Spartacus* or the 1959 *Ben-Hur*, where the movie-makers had to go to the expense of constructing arenas and peopling them with hundreds of extras. Now the whizz-kid on the computer summons all of this up with an intricate knowledge of how computer graphics work.

Yes, Hollywood has new toys and the danger is that the effects will swamp the end-product and that movies will try to outdo themselves in the audacity of the special effects produced. Yet perhaps this is just the complaint of a writer on film wedded to the old ways of doing things. Proponents of computer-generated effects would argue that movies such as *Toy Story* and *Toy Story 2*, far from being swamped by the special effects, are greatly enhanced by them because the story, characters and humour still shine through all the technological wizardry. Some serious people rate the two *Toy Story* movies as being among the best movies produced over the whole of the 1990s.

Similarly, the *Lord of the Rings* movies use an avalanche of special effects. Do these swamp the basic story of the search for the Ring? Or can the full impact of Tolkien's story only be communicated because of the wealth of special effects at the movie-makers' disposal? Is nothing to be left to the imagination of the audience by these spectacular effects? Should the audience be made to work harder to envisage for themselves the wonders of Tolkien's story? Are the special effects in essence the movie: a merging of style with meaning, so that the special effects are the meaning, the ultimate message of the film?

But I hear the cry that movies are just harmless entertainment. The intention behind movies such as *A Bug's Life, Antz, Shrek, Dinosaur* and *Stuart Little* is to provide an amusing entertainment for a couple of hours,

BELOW Antz (1998) is another computer-animated movie about an ant called Z with the voice and personality of Woody Allen.

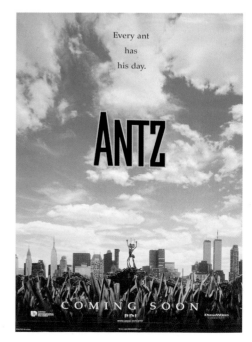
Every ant has his day.

ANTZ

COMING SOON

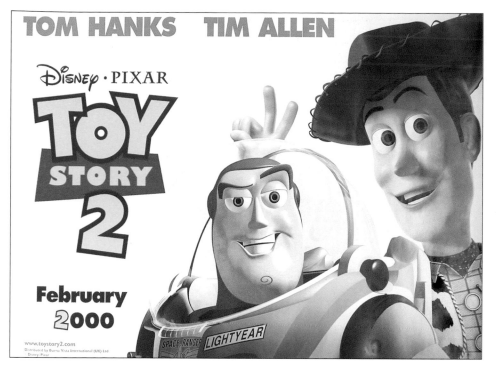

ABOVE Toy Story 2 (1999) is generally regarded as being even better than the 1995 Toy Story, and is also rated as the best of the new crop of computer-animated cartoons.

which will take the audience out of themselves and make them forget mundane reality for the period of time they are watching the screen. This is the way it has always been in the world of the cinema, and the advent of computer-generated effects has not really made any difference to that central aim of movies; it has merely expanded enormously the range and complexity of special effects that can be summoned up to keep an audience in that state of wonder that has been the aim of producers from the time of the nickelodeons onwards.

ABOVE Shrek (2001) had a sophisticated script, great computer-generated animation, together with the voices of Mike Myers, Eddie Murphy and Cameron Diaz, among others.

Well, perhaps. There will always be niche markets in world cinema and an audience for movies such as those of Ingmar Bergman and Krzysztof Kieslowski. Not all movies need to be festooned with special effects. The danger is that mainstream Hollywood movies, because of the enormous box-office receipts garnered by movies such as The Lord of the Rings and the Harry Potter series, all go for the same market and the same ingredients. There has always been a sort of territory between the extremes of the totally populist blockbusters and the art-house movies, inhabited by well-made, entertaining movies that are not insulting to the intelligence. Perhaps it is those kinds of movies that are threatened with extinction if everyone goes after the stupendous special-effects movie and their attendant big bucks. Meanwhile, computer-generated special effects movies are here to stay, and let's hope the movie-going public demand some sustenance for the brain while watching them and eating their popcorn. Mentally grazing while food-grazing is not to be recommended.

ABOVE The Lord of the Rings: The Fellowship of the Ring was an immense box-office hit and was generously rewarded with Oscars. The computer effects were even more sophisticated in the two sequels with the creation of the "CG" character, Gollum.

HOLLYWOOD SCANDALS AND TRAGEDIES

It is a hoary old cliché that Hollywood, and show-business in general, extracts a heavy price for its prizes of stardom and fame, but the history of the American film industry does seem to be littered with the dead bodies and ruined reputations of many of its most famous personalities. It may be that the movie industry extracts no higher price for success than, say, the profession of accountancy does, but suicides and murders among movie stars tend to reach the front pages rather more often.

Another matter of debate is how much these unfortunate stars were victims of an uncaring, exploitative system and how much they contributed to their own downfall through their own self-destructive natures. What is undoubtedly true is that people living under the glare of the Hollywood spotlights are at high risk of succumbing to egomania, self-destructive patterns, delusions, feelings of unworthiness and media hounding. "Ah, well," as the man said, "if you have the fame, you have to take the heartaches that go with it."

However, almost all spheres of endeavour in which the rewards are high in terms of fame, power and wealth cause casualties. In the world of politics, for example, reaching for the highest pinnacles of power means an individual lays himself or herself open to incredible scrutiny, and many a politician has crumbled under that gaze. But not many people weep over the corpses of politicians, so why should movie stars and film people gain more of our sympathy? Most people's attitude to the stars they admire are ambivalent: they admire from a distance, but some part of star

ABOVE *Rob Lowe's early exploits in his private life caused a stir in Hollywood, but they did not affect his film or television career.*

worship involves envy and the unconscious wish to destroy the loved one. The tabloid newspapers sell very well when they expose the scandals surrounding these gilded creatures who seem to have it all. Many people feel a certain guilty satisfaction in seeing the famous toppled. "See," they say, "they're just like the rest of us after all!" Well, of course they are. Movie stars are just actors elevated to almost mythical status, but they remain essentially Joe Bloggs from Idaho or Norma Nobody from Essex. And they make a mess of their lives just like you and me.

THE FATTY ARBUCKLE AFFAIR

In the very early days of Hollywood, Roscoe "Fatty" Arbuckle became a famous Mack Sennett slapstick comedian. He was a fat man with a moon face, and he had something on screen that made people laugh. He made two-reel silent comedies with titles such as *Fatty and Mabel's Simple Life*, *Mabel and Fatty's Married Life*, *Fatty's Flirtation* and *Fickle Fatty's Fall*. In other words, Arbuckle was a professional fat man, but he was a great box-office attraction and very well paid, until events that took place in 1921 put an end to his meteoric career.

The events that led to Arbuckle's downfall happened at a weekend-long party organized by Arbuckle in the St Francis Hotel in San Francisco. During the course of the party, a young starlet, Virginia Rappe, was severely injured around the abdomen: injuries that led to her death five days later from peritonitis. How she came to be seriously hurt was never finally established, but Arbuckle had been in a bedroom alone with her just before she was discovered in a state of severe pain and with her clothing torn. Rumours spread that Arbuckle had used a bottle on Rappe in a perverse and bizarre sexual attack.

Subsequently, Arbuckle was charged with rape and murder. The newspapers were full of the case and Arbuckle was tried and found guilty in the public consciousness before the case got anywhere near a court. The scandal rocked Hollywood, and the nation's moral guardians, eager to attack the film colony, labelled it a modern-day Sodom and Gomorrah. Further rumours circulated that

Arbuckle had used a Coca-Cola bottle on Rappe in an attempt at unnatural penetration. Three trials ensued and, after two hung juries (one opting for acquittal, the other for conviction), the third jury cleared Arbuckle of all charges. But his film career was over. Despite his acquittal, his erstwhile friends and the film studios turned their backs on him. He made a couple of two-reelers in the 1930s. The mighty had fallen and no one seemed to care very much. He had been found guilty by association. Arbuckle became an alcoholic and died at the

ABOVE *Fatty Arbuckle was a major star before his encounter with Virginia Rappe at a Hollywood party. Although he was never found guilty of any crime, the bad publicity effectively finished his movie career.*

age of 46 in 1933. Whether or not he was guilty (and after all he was innocent in the eyes of the law), Arbuckle's fall is a cautionary tale of excess and indulgence: sudden fame and riches can play havoc in the lives of ordinary people suddenly elevated to heights of fame and success that they had hitherto only dreamt of.

143

PAUL BERN AND JEAN HARLOW

Paul Bern was a top MGM executive in the 1930s. He was a small, unattractive man, hardly the type to be thought of as a likely husband for blonde star Jean Harlow, whose screen persona was brassy and promiscuous. However, Harlow had married Bern in July 1932. Perhaps she believed that a top executive such as Bern would help to protect her career at MGM; perhaps Bern, 22 years her senior, represented some kind of father figure for her. Whatever the reasons for the marriage, the couple appeared to be happy and the union seemed as likely to last as any other marriage in Tinsel Town, where even then the divorce rate was high.

But marital happiness, if they ever tasted any, did not last very long. Two months after the marriage Bern was found shot dead in their home. A suicide note was left in his handwriting, referring to his "abject humiliation" and to the previous night as "only a comedy". It seemed that Bern was so ashamed of his inability to make love to his wife that he took his own life. Whether this was because of Bern's homosexuality or some inadequacy in his sexual equipment has never really been clarified. It seemed, however, an open-and-shut case: little Paul Bern had taken his own life because he could not make love to his screen goddess wife.

Louis B. Mayer and Irving Thalberg, who ran MGM at that time, were on the scene before the police, giving rise to the rumour that some kind of cover-up had been put into operation. What did Mayer and Thalberg cook up between them to protect their star? Harlow was then a very "hot" property for the studio. Her pictures were making the studio millions of dollars, and she was young and seemed likely to remain a big star for a number of years. A lot was at stake.

The official story began to come out. It was stated that Harlow had been staying with her mother at the time of Bern's death. She had, of course, nothing to do with her husband's death. The couple were in love, but Bern had taken his own life while the balance of his mind was disturbed.

But was there more to this affair than met the eye? Could the suicide note have been forced out of Bern to make it look like suicide? Was Harlow actually there in the house at the time? Rumours abounded about Bern having found out about an affair that Harlow was having. The same rumours marked her down as her husband's killer and Mayer and Thalberg as perverting the course of justice to hide the real facts. Whatever the truth, Harlow herself did not survive her husband that long; by 1937 she too had died, from uremic poisoning.

BELOW *Jean Harlow was the epitome of sexual allure for 1930s audiences, so it was odd that insignificant-looking Paul Bern, an MGM executive, should be the man she chose to marry.*

ERROL FLYNN

Errol Flynn was a renowned womanizer on and off the screen, but his promiscuous ways landed him in deep trouble in 1942 when he was charged with statutory rape under a Californian law that made it illegal to have sex with anyone under the age of 18. At the Grand Jury hearing, Flynn was acquitted because the girls involved told conflicting stories. However, the authorities pursued the case and Flynn had to stand trial. Flynn had made some enemies in Hollywood, his lifestyle outraged the puritans and he was probably the most famous movie actor of his time: he had these three strikes against him, so there were lots of people out there gunning for him.

Jerry Geisler, a top-notch criminal lawyer, defended Flynn and managed to tear the girls' stories to shreds. Flynn was again acquitted. The real puzzle was: who or what was behind this campaign to get Flynn? A whole can of worms involving Warner Bros. and Flynn's studio paying kickbacks to politicians and the police could have been opened if anyone had spilled the beans. In other words, Flynn was almost certainly set up as a fall guy: his scalp would have been a feather in the cap of the investigating authorities. The possibility arises that the case collapsed because the authorities allowed it to collapse when his studio came to terms with the people who feared exposure. It was a grimy, corrupt mélange with powerful interests ranging up on both sides, and Flynn just happened to be the pinball being struck from side to side.

As it happened, Flynn's reputation as a lover and star was only enhanced by the trials. Unfortunately, his own self-destructive instincts saw to it that he departed this life at a comparatively young age without the help of outside agencies, apart from booze, drugs and a lifestyle that practically invited death. But, even after his death in 1959, they were still trying to pin something on old Errol: he has been variously accused of being a Nazi spy and an IRA supporter. Perhaps Flynn wasn't the only one who had difficulty in telling the difference between reality and the movies.

BELOW *Errol Flynn on location with co-star Olivia de Havilland during the shooting of the western* Dodge City *(1939).*

FRANCES FARMER

The story of Frances Farmer raises the issue of responsibility: was her steep fall from Hollywood grace largely self-inflicted, was she the victim of a vindictive system, or was it six of one and half-a-dozen of the other? Farmer was never a major star, but hers is an interesting case because she acquired a reputation for being a rebel within the Hollywood system. The question was: was she destroyed by that system or did she do it all herself?

Like other Hollywood luminaries such as John Garfield and Elia Kazan, Farmer had emerged from New York's Group Theatre, which had a reputation for being left-wing and challenging in theatrical terms. She was signed up by Paramount, but was used largely in extremely mediocre movies such as *Rhythm on the Range* (1936) and *South of Pago Pago* (1940). This may have been part of the

problem: she had come from the Group Theatre which had tried to mount meaningful plays with politically committed content; in Hollywood she was the love interest in Bing Crosby musicals.

Along the way she married a Hollywood actor, Leif Erickson, who, according to her, beat her up regularly. In 1943 she had a couple of dust-ups with the Los Angeles Police Department over traffic violations, then subsequently broke her parole. At her trial, she threw an ink-pot at the judge and slugged a police officer. She was put in a straitjacket, served some time in jail and a private sanatorium, then was committed for ten years to a state asylum where she was systematically abused and humiliated. Finally, she had a lobotomy, which left her stable but unrecognizable. When she was released from the asylum she even

ABOVE *Frances Farmer looking relaxed and composed: a publicity photograph taken before her breakdown. The Hollywood publicity machine ignored the reality of stars' lives.*

fronted a television show for a while. Her story was filmed in 1983 with Jessica Lange playing her.

Farmer was undoubtedly a strong-minded, independent woman with left-wing sympathies. This combination probably accounts in part for the horrific treatment that was doled out to her. Had she been star in Hollywood in the 1960s rather than in the 30s, her form of spirited independence might have been accommodated. As it was, in the 40s when her real troubles began, the powers-that-be were unaccustomed to dealing with young women who refused to conform and who were not over-grateful for getting trashy parts in tenth-rate movies.

LANA TURNER AND THE HOOD

As a young 17-year-old Hollywood hopeful, Lana Turner had supposedly been discovered by a press agent sitting in Schwabs Drugstore on Sunset Boulevard. Like many of the myths surrounding this actress, this was complete hogwash. Nevertheless, Turner quickly became a star for reasons that leave some of us bewildered. She couldn't act, sing or dance, and her looks were of the plastic variety. By the time she became headline news again because of a murder case, her career was in decline, but along the way she had been a major box-office star.

In 1958, Lana Turner's daughter Cheryl stabbed to death her mother's lover, Johnny Stompanato, in her mother's bedroom in the Beverly Hills mansion that the three of them shared. Stompanato, a psychopath with gangland connections, had repeatedly threatened Turner during the course of their relatively brief relationship. Cheryl, 14 at the time of the killing, had overheard the "gigolo-type" Stompanato threatening to cut her mother up. She then took a long kitchen knife and plunged it into his stomach.

At the subsequent trial, Turner reputedly gave one of her best performances: as the distraught and contrite mother fighting for her daughter. The jury returned a verdict of justifiable homicide. However, the details of Turner's private life were splashed over every front page in America. Some vindictive people released her love letters to Stompanato to the press. The strong rumour started that it had been Turner herself who had stabbed Stompanato in a lovers' quarrel and that her daughter had taken the rap because of the certain knowledge that she would be acquitted. The irony is that, after all this bad publicity, Turner's career

had an upsurge and she continued to make films, one of which – *Imitation of Life* – was her greatest success. The connections between Hollywood and organized crime have never been a secret as such, but the Turner–Stompanato affair brought some of those tawdry connections to the fore.

ABOVE *Life imitated the movies when Lana Turner was involved in a real-life murder case. Her Hollywood career did not suffer, however, and she later starred in Sirk's appropriately titled* Imitation of Life (1959).

147

GEORGE CUKOR, CLARK GABLE AND
GONE WITH THE WIND

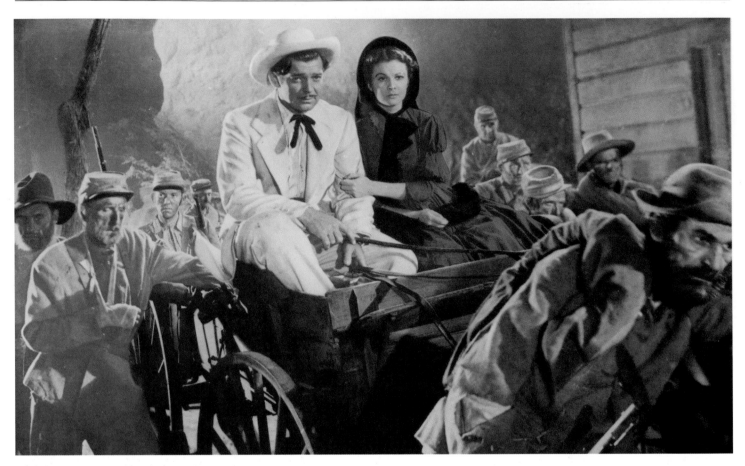

In 1939 George Cukor was assigned to direct *Gone with the Wind* by producer David Selznick. It was a dream assignment because even before it came in front of the cameras *GWTW* was the most talked-about movie ever. Cukor, one of Hollywood's most discreet homosexuals, had made his reputation by directing female stars (Hepburn, Garbo and Crawford) in *Dinner at Eight*, *Little Women* and *Sylvia Scarlett*. Insiders in Hollywood and in the Hollywood press corps must have known about Cukor's homosexuality, but there was a code of silence about it. Nowadays, no one would raise an eyebrow in Hollywood if a director announced to the world that he was gay, but those were different times. As long as Cukor remained discreet, so would the press. (However, Cukor was himself a notorious gossip.)

Shortly after filming on *Gone with the Wind* commenced, Selznick replaced Cukor with Victor Fleming, a journeyman MGM director. Seemingly, Clark Gable – Rhett Butler in the film – had insisted that Cukor be replaced because the star felt that Cukor was too much of a woman's director and was giving undue attention to Vivien Leigh in her role as Scarlett O'Hara, and too little to Gable and the male side of the story. That was the official reason given for replacing Cukor. It says much about the power of a major star like Gable that he could pull strings to replace a director in the middle of a shoot and on such a major, major production as *GWTW*. But when it came down to it, in a battle of wills, there was no contest between Gable and Cukor. Selznick and MGM needed Gable; they did not need Cukor as much.

ABOVE *Clark Gable in his most famous role as Rhett Butler. Could the most masculine of Hollywood stars really have had a spell as a rent-boy, as director George Cukor claimed?*

Near the end of his life, however, Cukor gave quite a different explanation for his replacement. According to Cukor, before Gable had become a star, he had been an up-market rent-boy for Hollywood's homosexual colony. Gable was aware that Cukor knew this sordid detail about him and could not bear to be directed by the man. Thus, he insisted that Cukor be given the push. By the time Cukor made these allegations, Gable had been dead nearly 30 years, so it may have been the act of a vindictive old queen, getting his own back on the star who had had him sacked all those years ago by making up nasty stories about Gable's youth.

THE STRANGE OBSESSIONS OF ALFRED HITCHCOCK

Hitchcock's obsession with cool, blonde women, such as Grace Kelly, Kim Novak and Ingrid Bergman, was well known, but the extent to which he carried this neurotic attachment with another of his stars, Tippi Hedren, was disturbing to say the least. Hedren starred in two of Hitchcock's movies, *Marnie* and *The Birds*, the latter being about the sudden inexplicable onslaught by our feathered friends on a small fishing village. An ex-model, Hedren was perhaps a surprising choice to take the female lead in these two movies, because both parts demanded a range of emotional acting skills she had given no evidence of before on screen. At best she is barely adequate in both movies.

For some of the scenes in *The Birds*, Hitchcock insisted that real birds be used to peck away at Hedren while she was pinned down by invisible bonds. She was protected by a net that would not show up on film, but clearly the scenes involved more than a little risk to Hitchcock's new star. After a week-long shooting of a particular scene, things got wildly out of hand. Hedren was reduced to hysteria after remorseless attacks by crazed birds, and she also suffered a severe injury to one of her eyes.

The evidence suggests that Hitchcock was undoubtedly strongly sexually attracted to her, a feeling that was not reciprocated. Perhaps the director represented his anger at being repulsed by the actress in these elongated scenes of ornithological assault. It seems that Hitchcock was eaten up with self-loathing because of his obesity and took it out on blonde actresses who aroused his hopeless passions. If this is the case, it is all rather sad. In Hitchcock's defence, he went to meticulous lengths to achieve the effects he wanted to put on celluloid. He saw his job as making the audience squirm with anxiety. Perhaps his zeal in setting up the bird attack scenes on Hedren was more to do with the director's pursuit of screen perfection. I would say the jury is still out on this one.

BELOW *Alfred Hitchcock had a thing about cool blondes. Eva Marie Saint starred in his excellent 1958 thriller,* North by Northwest.

GIG YOUNG

No screen persona belied the reality of an actor's life more than that adopted by Gig Young. Young had a long movie career as a light comedian, playing the hero's best friend, the charming rival of the star and the second lead who never seemed to get the girl in movies such as *Old Acquaintance, Young at Heart, Desk Set, Ask Any Girl, That Touch of Mink* and *Strange Bedfellows*. On screen, he seemed to be the eternal philandering bachelor without a care in the world and living the life of Reilly. His features revealed an inner soul untroubled by anxieties. In real life, however, Young was an alcoholic, and in the latter part of his life he suffered from skin cancer. Many actors are like Young: on the surface they are happy-go-lucky, affable, seemingly making their way through life like blessed children. Under this superficial front, however, they are a mass of insecurities. Acting is their way of covering up their distress.

In 1978 at the age of 64 and with his screen career in decline, Young married a woman of 31. Only three weeks later both of them were found dead in his New York apartment. Young was clutching a revolver. The obvious conclusion was that Young had first shot his wife in the head, then turned the gun on himself. Whether his wife was party to a suicide pact or not remains in doubt.

The carefree actor in some of Hollywood's lightest confections had faced up to the desperation of his own life and put an end to it, taking his new wife with him. Movies create illusions: about ourselves, about the stars we see on the screen, and about what is perceived as reality. In the case of Gig Young, the escape he found in the illusions of the screen was no longer enough of a safety net. He ended those illusions with a bullet to his head.

LEFT *In this studio pose Gig Young is the debonair actor the world saw on screen, but behind that carefree air was a deeply insecure man. When the aging process caught up with him, he could not face his life any more.*

THE LOVING MOTHER

In 1977 Christina Crawford, Joan Crawford's adopted daughter, wrote a memoir about her mother entitled *Mommie Dearest*. It chronicled a story of the Crawford family life as vicious and uncaring. Up there on the silver screen Joan Crawford so often played the sacrificial mother fighting her way to the top to give the good things of life to her children. In real life, Crawford seemingly acquired her two adopted children because it would help her image as a caring star and hence her film career, which had gone into decline. She imposed severe discipline on the kids, beating them with coathangers amongst other things, and expecting absurd levels of obedience and regimentation.

Crawford had always worked hard at her career in her younger years, seeking sugar daddies who were in a position to land her the small parts that were essential if she was to climb the stairway to stardom. Eventually, by sheer determination rather than talent, she became a featured player, then an MGM star. Stories abound in Hollywood about her legendary bitchiness, especially to other female stars such as Norma Shearer, Greta Garbo and Bette Davis. When she could no longer play ambitious secretaries, she turned to playing suffering matrons. Throughout her career she pandered to the fan magazines and in public played the role of the star to the hilt.

Crawford's adopted children were forced to pose with her for loving family publicity pictures, which disguised the hell they were living through. The final straw for daughter Christina was when her mother took over her role in a television soap opera when she (Christina) was lying ill in hospital. Seeing her mother play a part – her part – that was meant for an actress 40 years younger probably

finally prompted Christina to write *Mommie Dearest*. It was filmed in 1981 with Faye Dunaway playing Crawford. As someone who courted fame and publicity assiduously all her life, Crawford might not have been too unhappy at this late burst of fame. In 1938 she had been one of the stars dubbed "box-office poison" in an

ABOVE *Joan Crawford, at the height of her phenomenal success as a movie star, in* The Shining Hour *(1938).*

ad placed by exhibitors in The Hollywood Reporter. She fought her way back from that nadir and would have clawed her way back after *Mommie Dearest*, had she not died in 1977.

151

COLLECTING MOVIE MEMORABILIA

The collecting of movie memorabilia expanded spectacularly in the 1990s, once the major auction houses realized there were people out there willing to pay good money for vintage movie posters, costumes and props, star autographs and a whole range of other collectables. What had been a small niche market for avid movie fans who frequented movie jumbles and scoured "collectables" shops suddenly burgeoned into a collecting area that rivalled other similar pastimes such as acquiring rock memorabilia or modern first editions of novels.

There are all sorts of reasons why collectors want movie "trash". Vintage movie posters are the main target for most collectors and they may want to build a collection around a genre (westerns, *film noir*, musicals, British comedy, sci-fi and horror). Or some people collect on a particular star or director, so they will want to acquire

every movie poster relating to their idol. What they want are the first-release movie posters that were issued at the time of the movies' initial screening. Whether or not a movie poster is from a first release or a later reissue makes a great difference to the value of a poster, just as the first edition of a novel is worth more than subsequent reprints. And, of course, these are genuine movie posters, not the kind of commercial reprints that are sold by poster shops, which have no intrinsic value. Each country produces their own posters for individual movies, so a keen collector of the Orson Welles movie *Touch of Evil*, say, would want to acquire the original US, British, French, Italian, German, Polish, Spanish, Argentinian, Belgian and other countries' posters for that movie.

Original movie props from films such as the *Star Wars* series or Universal horror movies go for a tidy sum, and costumes that stars have worn on screen also fetch high prices. What people are buying is a part of screen history, and acquiring a prop or costume brings them closer to the movie world that fascinates them. Original stills, lobby cards, the press books that the studios sent out to exhibitors and journalists, autographs, movie

ABOVE *Sci-fi movie posters from the 1950s are highly valued by collectors. This poster for* The Day the Earth Stood Still *(1951) typifies the quality of graphic art that is most prized by collectors.*

magazines, ads and flyers: these are some of the other collecting areas that fuel the market.

So how valuable are some old vintage movie posters, for example? The world record for a movie poster sold at auction belongs to an original US one sheet of the 1932 *The Mummy*.

LEFT *An original US movie poster for* The Mummy *holds the world record for a movie poster sold at auction. Its rarity explains the price.*

RIGHT *Original James Bond movie posters have shot up in value since the 1990s, and the Bond craze shows no sign of abating.*

ABOVE, RIGHT AND BELOW *Avid collectors will try to acquire all the posters issued for their particular favourite. Here we have three different posters for* The Italian Job: *the American, Japanese and British posters.*

ABOVE *Breakfast at Tiffany's is a favourite target for movie poster collectors. This is one of the original Italian posters for the movie.*

It was bought by one happy collector for $453,500 in 1997. Indeed, 1930s Universal horror posters figure prominently in the all-time record lists. Anything original on the 1933 *King Kong* also fetches very high prices: $244,500 in 1999 for an original US one sheet. Fritz Lang's *Metropolis* is also highly sought after: $357,750 in 2000 for an original German poster. *Casablanca, Gone with the Wind, Citizen Kane,* very early Disney or RKO musicals, and the *James Bond* movies (the Sean Connery titles) are other areas that invariably attract high prices.

So, with prices like those around, it is clear that the unwary could get their fingers burnt by buying the wrong item at an inflated price. The internet, and especially auction sites such as *eBay,* have thrown fuel on the craze for collecting movie memorabilia. On any given day, there are hundreds of thousands of items of movie memorabilia for sale on *eBay* alone. And then there are dealers in movie memorabilia from many countries who advertise items for sale through their websites. Specialist galleries have sprung up in major cities such as London, New York, Los Angeles and Paris. Auction houses such as Christie's and Sotheby's hold regular sales of movie items, and some auction houses also sell through internet bidding. If you really want to start a collection, then there is an Aladdin's Cave out there to feast on.

A very useful guide to the value of movie posters is provided by *The Movie Poster Price Almanac.* Edited by John Kisch, it is updated annually and gives inclusive lists of the price of posters of almost every film ever made, as recorded from sales at auction, through dealers' websites or via *eBay.* Information about this invaluable guide is available from *info@posterprice.com.* Good hunting!

ENDQUOTES

"I started at the top
and worked down."
ORSON WELLES

"To put it bluntly, I seem to
be a whole superstructure
without a foundation, but I am
working on the foundation."
MARILYN MONROE

"I never hear anyone say, boy,
I must see that film, I hear it
came in under budget."
BILLY WILDER

"The thing about Larry was he was
jealous of everyone, whatever they
did, if he felt they did whatever
they did better than he could. This
gnawing dissatisfaction made him
terribly unhappy all his life."
*ROBERT STEPHENS ON
LAURENCE OLIVIER*

"To make a film is to improve on
life, to arrange it to suit oneself, to
prolong the games of childhood,
to construct something which is at
once a new toy and a vase in which
one can arrange in a permanent way
the ideas one feels in the morning."
FRANÇOIS TRUFFAUT

"I was the only star they allowed to
come out of the water looking wet."
BETTE DAVIS

"I never go out unless I look like
Joan Crawford, the movie star.
If you want to see the girl next
door, go next door."
JOAN CRAWFORD

"I'm revered like an old building.
Yet I still seem to be master of
my fate. The boat may only be
a canoe, but I'm paddling it."
KATHARINE HEPBURN

"I don't use any particular
method. I'm from the let's
pretend school of acting."
HARRISON FORD

"The tougest three pictures I ever
made. It was shot in a state of
emergency, shot in confusion,
and wound up in blind panic."
JOSEPH L. MANKIEWICZ ON CLEOPATRA

"I sometimes think I'm impersonating
the dark unconscious of the whole
human race. I know this sounds
sick, but I love it."
VINCENT PRICE

"I've got a very good left profile
and a very bad right profile. I was
the Loretta Young of my day.
I was only ever photographed
on the left-hand profile."
DIRK BOGARDE

"I've never been through psycho-
analysis. I solve my problems
through the pictures I make."
STEVEN SPIELBERG

"At heart Larry was what the French
call a *cabotin*. Not exactly a ham:
a performer, a vulgarian, someone
who lives and dies for acting."
*DIRECTOR TONY RICHARDSON ON
LAURENCE OLIVIER*

"I have life rage. What am I going to
do with it? I can't kick the shit out of
someone. I have a therapist on each
coast. I've had a different personality
when I go to each one."
CHRISTINA RICCI

"I'M NO ACTOR AND I'VE 64 PICTURES TO PROVE IT."
VICTOR MATURE

"I DON'T ASK QUESTIONS. I JUST TAKE THEIR MONEY AND
USE IT FOR THINGS THAT REALLY INTEREST ME."
GEORGE SANDERS

"Hollywood, like Midas,
kills whatever it touches."
*CLIFFORD ODETS, DRAMATIST
AND SCREENWRITER*

"I don't care to belong to any
social organization which would
accept me as a member."
GROUCHO MARX

"Can you imagine being overpaid for
dressing up and playing games?"
DAVID NIVEN

"I do not believe the public will want
spoken comedy. Motion pictures and
the spoken arts are two distinct arts."
HAROLD LLOYD, SILENT ERA COMEDIAN

"My acting range? Left eyebrow
raised, right eyebrow raised."
ROGER MOORE

"Writing a good movie brings
a writer about as much fame
as steering a bicycle."
BEN HECHT

"I've been to Paris, France, and
I've been to Paris, Paramount.
Paris, Paramount is better."
*ERNST LUBITSCH, WRITER
AND DIRECTOR*

"Charlie Chaplin is no
businessman – all he knows is
he can't take anything less."
SAMUEL GOLDWYN

"He's about as likely a candidate
for stardom as the neighbourhood
delicatessen man."
TIME MAGAZINE ON WALTER MATTHAU

"I live by a man's code designed
to fit a man's world, yet at the
same time I never forget that a
woman's first job is to choose
the right shade of lipstick."
CAROLE LOMBARD

"I am paid not to think."
CLARK GABLE

"She moves rigidly on to the set,
as if wheels were concealed under
the stately skirt; she says her piece
with flat dignity and trolleys out
again, rather like a mechanical
marvel from the World's Fair."
*GRAHAM GREENE ON BRITISH ACTRESS
ANNA NEAGLE*

"Strip the phoney tinsel off
Hollywood and you'll find
the real tinsel underneath."
OSCAR LEVANT

"The number one book of the
age was written by a committee,
and it was called the Bible."
LOUIS B. MAYER

"Acting has been good to
me. It has taken me to play
golf all over the world."
BORIS KARLOFF

"Motivation is a lot of crap."
DEAN MARTIN

"The days at MGM were marvellous.
Everyone was pitching in. We had
real collaboration. It was fun.
We didn't think it was work."
GENE KELLY

"IF I'M WORKING WITH FRIGHTENED PEOPLE, I DO TEND TO DOMINATE THEM.
I'M NO DOLL, THAT'S FOR SURE."
BURT LANCASTER

INDEX

157

ACKNOWLEDGEMENTS

The publisher would like to thank the following for the use of their pictures:

Cine Art Gallery
759 Fulham Road
London SW6 5UU

Vertigo Gallery
29 Bedfordbury
Covent Garden
London WC2N 4BJ

Moviedrome
moviedrome@ntlworld.com